The Win-Win

of

Divine Greatness

THE SECRETS OF MASTERING THE WINNING EDGE

Dr. Y. Bur

Available Titles

ASITPLEASESGOD.COM

THE WIN-WIN OF DIVINE GREATNESS

THE SECRETS OF MASTERING THE WINNING EDGE

Copyright © 2021 by R.O.A.R. Publishing Group. All rights reserved.

Visit www.RoarPublishingGroup.com for more information. No part of this publication may be reproduced, stored in a retrieval system, or transmitted in any way by any means, electronic, mechanical, photocopy, recording, or otherwise, without the prior permission of the author except as provided by USA copyright law.

R.O.A.R. Publishing Group
581 N. Park Ave. Ste. #725
Apopka, FL 32704
ROAR-58-2316
762-758-2316

www.RoarPublishingGroup.com
Dr.YBur@gmail.com

Send Questions or Comments to:
CustomerService@RoarPublishingGroup.com

Published in the United States of America
ISBN: 978-1-948936-52-1
$22.88

Please Send Prayers, Testimonies, Donations, or Orders to:

Dr. Y. Bur
R.O.A.R. Publishing Group
581 N. Park Ave. Ste. #725
Apopka, FL 32704
ROAR-58-2316
762-758-2316
Dr.YBur@gmail.com

Visit Us At:
 AsItPleasesGodMovement
 AsItPleasesGod

 DrYBur.com
AsItPleasesGod.com

Please Donate

Please DONATE to this *Missionable Movement of God* as a GIVE-BACK to the Kingdom. Thanks for your support. Many Blessings.

AIPG Donation Link

Scan to Pay

Table of Contents

Introduction 7
Chapter One 11
   DNA of a *Win-Win* 11
Chapter Two 17
   Winning Edge 17
Chapter Three 25
   Seed Power 25
Chapter Four 35
   Situational *Win-Wins* 35
Chapter Five 45
   TRIP SWITCH 45
Chapter Six 55
   Spiritual Principles 55
Chapter Seven 63
   New Beginnings 63
Chapter Eight 71
   Actionable Behaviors 71
Chapter Nine 79
   What is Mind Mapping? 79
Chapter Ten 91
   Smart Moves 91

Chapter Eleven 99
    Mental Muscles 99
Chapter Twelve 111
    Platform of Greatness 111

INTRODUCTION

The *Winning Edge* is hidden within everyone, even if we seem to be on a losing streak. According to the Heavenly of Heavens, the edge we seek is only a Mindset away from allowing us to reap our greatest harvest, especially if we dare to allow it to do what it is Divinely Designed to do. After all, our Blueprint of Greatness has already been written. We only need to elevate ourselves to reverse our wrongs to rights by taking a journey within to help ourselves without pointing the finger at what is wrong.

Unbeknown to most, we can better pinpoint the *Win-Win* within ourselves by making a conscious effort to understand what is RIGHT with ourselves and others. However, this results from having a Trained Mindset to EXTRACT and CONVERT the information and experiences the way God intended from the BEGINNING.

In this book, we will take a journey within the DNA of the *Win-Win* to give us a bird's eye view of its *Genetic Design* according to the Standards of the Kingdom, *As It Pleases God*. Then again, we can tiptoe around the desires associated with becoming a WINNER. Still, the Power of our Seeds will not lie. They want to germinate even if we do not understand the process of doing so. For this reason, we will lay out the format on how to create a *Win-Win* with the least amount of effort and the most effective approaches according to Kingdom Standards.

In the Covenantal Agreement from the Heavenly of Heavens, regardless of who does or does not like us or what we are doing, it does not stop our *Win-Win*. When our *Win-Win* is according to our Divine Blueprint, no one can circumvent its UNVEILING, unless we do. In essence, no one can stop God, but we can knowingly or unknowingly stop or block ourselves.

When we allow Mental, Physical, Emotional, or Spiritual Blocks into our lives, if we are not careful, they will cause known and unknown missed opportunities and Blessings. Once we are on the losing end or passed over all the time, if we do not know how to create a *Win-Win*, it contributes to us coveting another man's possessions or accomplishments. Or, it may zap our desire to put in the inner work to possess our own.

Unbeknownst to many of us, everything we need to succeed is already ingrained in our Divine Blueprint. To get to this point, we must be vigilant in identifying and removing any negative barriers that cloud our vision, hinder our understanding, and prevent us from recognizing the abundant potential lying within. By doing so, we can unlock our true potential and achieve great things in life.

When we take complete responsibility for our *Situational Win-Wins* and outcomes, we are better able to pinpoint what is hidden under the smokescreens designed to deceive, derail, or deter us.

More importantly, we must also become aware of our *Trip Switches* to keep ourselves from becoming negatively triggered. According to the Heavenly of Heavens, knowing our triggers allows us to approach challenges with a positive and proactive attitude, leading to more favorable results for everyone involved, *As It Pleases God*.

Above all, pinpointing our triggers also prevents us from doing an about-face in the wrong direction or becoming rejected because we have openly tripped out. In the Eye of God, making excuses or selfishly justifying our behaviors prevents us from taking responsibility for our actions, reactions, thoughts, words, beliefs, and biases. This internal glitch also prevents us from finding ways to improve and become better, stronger, and wiser. Nevertheless, to remain on the *Winning Edge*, it is essential to recognize our mistakes and shortcomings so that we can learn from them and make positive changes as we move forward in the Spirit of Excellence, *As It Pleases God*.

What if we are stuck between a rock and a hard place? I would say, 'Do not leave any stone unturned!' When we are secretly lost from within or aimlessly wandering in our private desert, the drought has a way of putting a damper on our *Win-Win*. In addition, it also causes us to badmouth ourselves and others. Not realizing it takes the same amount of energy to do good, reverse the fruits of our lips, or use the *Spiritual Principles* readily available to promote a *New Beginning* from the inside out, without losing hope.

Now, from one *Win-Win* to another, according to the Heavenly of Heavens, we have what it takes to regraft our lives. All we need to do is invoke the Gravitational Pull of a *Winning Mindset*. So, if we take a little time to focus on our *Actionable Behaviors*, we will better understand the root of our fruits and where the regrafting or pruning process must occur.

From the Ancient of Days, no one is exempt from working on themselves, *As It Pleases God*, even if we somehow pretend we are. Still, as we become a work-in-progress, *As It Pleases Him*, everyone does not know what to do when faced with the conversion method needed to create *Win-Win Situations* consistently and effectively. Please, let this not be you. If you are ready, willing, and able, let us do this together as One, getting to the nitty-gritty, empowering the Grace of God to fall fresh on you. Yes, you! The time is now to do what He has designed according to the Divine Blueprint set forth from the BEGINNING of your inception.

The truth is: You are here for a reason, the Divine Mission has not changed, and the show must go on. What is intricately woven into the fabric of your existence is still there, waiting for your cue of readiness. Even with the twists and turns, the challenges and triumphs, or the self-induced and man-orchestrated fiery furnaces, you are not an accident, failure, or mistake. The Winning Greatness hidden within your loins must come forth as pure gold. The bottom line is that the Kingdom of God needs your tailored experiences, lessons, skills, and know-how.

As Dr. Y. Bur, The WHY Doctor, I am here to remind you that you are a Winner, you are Divine, and you are Great. In a world filled with unavoidable challenges and uncertainties, it is my reasonable service to share with you the secrets I learned on my Spiritual Journey with executable roadmaps, charts, and zero fluff...Just results!

With all simplicity, like a Diamond in the Rough, deep within each of you lies a powerful truth that only you can tap into, unleashing the Divine Greatness, which is already. This proven Do-It-Yourself, *As It Pleases God*, transformative process is designed to elevate your Mind, Body, Soul, and Spirit, positively impacting your life and the lives of those around you. Together, we will explore the profound significance of your existence and the remarkable impact you can make in the world in real time.

Your Divine Destiny is calling. Will you awaken from your slumber, take ownership, and answer the call? Or, will you hang up or remain asleep with doubt, comparison, competitiveness, jealousy, envy, pride, and ungratefulness flowing through your veins? All of these negative attributes come with the territory of being out of purpose and lacking passion. Really? Yes, really!

From me to you, your Divine Greatness is not merely for your personal gain, benefit, or edification. It is Divinely Designed to be positively shared with the world for the Greater Good of mankind. The moment you allow your true self to shine or come forth as TRUE LIGHT, *As It Pleases God*, it inspires others to do likewise, creating a ripple effect of growth, empowerment, and transformation, similar to what I am doing right now. So, without further ado, let's bring forth the Winning Greatness hidden within you.

Chapter One

DNA OF A *WIN-WIN*

The possibilities of finding a *Win-Win* are significantly increased when we understand its DNA process. The DNA of a *Win-Win* is unique to how we are individually prewired, similar to a Seed bearing whatever is in its DNA Structure without deviation. Although we do not think about it much, we are the same. We merely do not realize it because we have not mastered its use or the process of conveyance.

According to the Heavenly of Heavens, we are prewired, predestined, or predesigned to WIN whether we are in or out of the Kingdom of God. Now, before we go any further, here is what we need to know: *"Now when He was asked by the Pharisees when the Kingdom of God would come, He answered them and said, 'The Kingdom of God does not come with observation; nor will they say, 'See here!' or 'See there!' For indeed, the Kingdom of God is within you.' "* Luke 17:20-21. So, what is in our DNA? The Kingdom!

We are not created as losers; this is a conditioned or manipulated mindset. The moment we are conceived in the womb, the winning process begins. Unfortunately, if the conditions are not right, it will RESET the environmental womb by Divine Default. On the other hand, if the conditions are right, we become a newborn, breathing the Breath of Life, which is the greatest *Win-Win* of all.

The second greatest *Win-Win* is when we are born again back into the Realm of the Spirit, breathing the Breath of the Kingdom. How is this possible? *"Jesus answered and said to him, 'Most assuredly, I say to you, unless one is born again, he cannot see the Kingdom of God.' Nicodemus said to Him, 'How can a man be born when he is old? Can he enter a second time into his mother's womb and be born?' Jesus answered, 'Most assuredly, I say to you, unless one is born of water and the Spirit, he cannot enter the Kingdom of God. That which is born of the flesh is flesh, and that which is born of the Spirit is Spirit. Do not marvel that I said to you, 'You must be born again.'"* John 3:3-7.

As It Pleases God, our bodies are naturally designed to create a pathway of *Win-Wins* on our behalf to keep us alive, even when we secretly or openly give up. Well, the *Win-Win* of Life is designed to do likewise; thus, we must put in the work to pay attention. What do we need to look for? It will vary from person to person, situation to situation, condition to condition, Blueprint to Blueprint, and so on. However, once again, we must learn how to ask the right fact-finding questions in the *What, When, Where, How, Why,* and with *Whom* Formation while documenting accordingly.

If we are having a hard time doing a *Q and A Session* on ourselves, it only means that we have a lot of debris, toxins, or untruths residing in the human psyche. But it is still doable if we persist without giving up on the process or ourselves. What is the purpose of knowing this information? It helps us to align our behaviors, attitudes, demeanors, words, actions, thoughts, and beliefs with the Fruits of the Spirit and Christlike Character to empower our SEEDS or DEEDS with the Spirit of Righteousness. If not, misalignment takes place, tainting our underlying fruits or contaminating our roots.

What do our fruits and roots have to do with our *Win-Wins*? They are essential because they branch out to all other areas from the inside out, governing our flow of wisdom, understanding, counsel, knowledge, and so on, from the Realm of the Spirit.

Nevertheless, according to Isaiah 11:1-2, "*There shall come forth a Rod from the stem of Jesse, and a Branch shall grow out of his roots. The Spirit of the LORD shall rest upon Him, The Spirit of wisdom and understanding, The Spirit of counsel and might, The Spirit of knowledge and of the fear of the LORD.*"

Our developmental abilities are intertwined in our DNA. If we have a desire to capitalize on our Divine Design, we must understand how it will work on our behalf without interjecting all types of worldliness into what is Spiritual. What does this mean? We are Spiritual Beings having a human experience. Respecting our Earthen Vessels in such a manner allows our Winning DNA to avail itself, especially when we put a demand on it.

For example, we are like a SEED planted on Earth to have a Heaven on Earth Experience. Still, we must become Spiritually Watered by the Heavenly of Heavens to produce the anticipated Spiritual Fruits feeding the Experience. If we turn away from the Heavenly Source of hydration or nutrition, we will begin to thirst and hunger from the inside out. We contradict the anticipated design or genetic makeup; as a result, the DNA of the *Win-Win* becomes compromised or confused. Once this happens, it will shut down or attempt to RESET itself. Frankly, this is one of the reasons why we feel the inner struggle from within, especially when we are out of the Will of God.

When dealing with the *DNA of a Win-Win*, it is our responsibility to lay the foundation or groundwork needed to sustain our *Win-Wins* or defeats appearing real. Suppose we cannot handle being on the Winning Edge or suffering a temporary loss, Mentally, Physically, Emotionally, or Spiritually. In this case, we will find ourselves in a state of self-sabotage without realizing what we are doing to ourselves or the people around us. Listen, in the Kingdom, being that we are trapped in time, the Cycle of Life will cause us to '*lose to win*' and '*win to lose*' based upon the Spiritual Principles of Seedtime and Harvest.

No one is 100% right or wrong all the time, and we all make mistakes; however, it does not mean we cannot reverse a negative situation into a positive one. For this reason, we must understand that *Win-Win* is a MINDSET of looking for the good in all things, ushering us into our Birthrights, Blessings, Provisions, and Divine Favor.

Furthermore, if the truth is told, if we are NOT operating with a Kingdom Mindset or a Positive Mental Attitude, being on the losing end of life does not make us comfortable at all. Actually, it irritates us, causing us to pick up bad habits contributing to our condition. Or, it may add fuel to the fire, creating a consuming combustion of our challenges, getting soot on everyone getting close to us. Therefore, on this day, the contradictory behaviors must come to a halt, allowing us to understand some of the charactorial behaviors, habits, decisions, and fruits causing the simulation or perception of defeat.

Why do we need to know about our contradictory behaviors? If we do not know this information for ourselves, who is going to reveal it to us? We must conduct our own inner queries to expose the self-defiant characteristics or habits, regrafting them according to the Standards or Principles of the Kingdom, *As It Pleases God*. If not, we will find ourselves trying to win approval from others instead of creating a *Winning Environment* within the human psyche.

The bottom line is that we must learn how to overcome, understand, and deal with our obstacles, setbacks, or challenges without allowing our outside distractions to provide solutions that do not fit our situation. What is the big deal? Detailed instructions are not provided, nor do they assist in identifying the ROOT or SEED of the issue.

According to the Heavenly of Heavens, seeking approval and praise from others should not be our primary focus. We will set ourselves up for disappointment when we do not get the expected accolades or support. For this reason, the goal of this book is to target our *Win-Wins* from within, spreading outwardly, taking the pressure off of people while placing a Spiritual Demand on the Holy Trinity due to the origin of our DNA. Can we really do this? Absolutely! Unbeknown to most, it is a part of our Divine Birthright.

As It Pleases God: Book Series

Remember, when Spiritually Capitalizing, *As It Pleases God*, as a formal disclosure to all, this is a free will event. Why must this be mentioned? When dealing with Spiritual Laws, Principles, Concepts, and Covenants, I cannot force this upon anyone; they must want it for themselves while Spiritually Tilling their own ground. Then again, if they want to remain in their condition, they have the right to do so. Therefore, they cannot pass the buck or lay the blame elsewhere. What if they do? It will NOT be justified in the Eye of God. Now, regardless of what decision we make, here is what we need to know, but not limited to such:

- ☐ With God, all things are possible.
- ☐ With God, there is no limit to what we can achieve.
- ☐ With God, we have what it takes.
- ☐ With God, we have a way out of worldliness and into the Kingdom.
- ☐ With God, we can become better, greater, knowledgeable, astute, and wiser.
- ☐ With God, the fight is fixed; we have the right to pick up our Spiritual Crown and walk in Greatness.
- ☐ With God, we can begin again, regardless of what we have done or what we have been through.
- ☐ With God, we are never alone.
- ☐ With God, love will never fail us.
- ☐ With God, His Promises are readily available.
- ☐ With God, we are His prized possession.
- ☐ With the Holy Trinity, the *Win-Win* is at our beck and call once we usher in the MINDSET of the Kingdom.

As the Ancient of Days are among us, regardless of where we are in life or what we are doing, all hope is not lost. Once we get a full understanding of how to graft the Mind of God into ours, we will find the thermostat of the *Win-Win* must keep us on the *Winning Edge* by Divine Default. The moment we begin to STAND for the Kingdom of Heaven without wavering in faith, it will STAND up on our behalf, ushering us into the *Win-Wins* we did not see coming.

The truth of the matter is that we do not have to create *Win-Wins* independently; we have help. In my opinion, we should take advantage of the Divine Assistance available to us, even when we cannot have our way. What is the use, especially when it is not on our terms? Let me answer this question with another. If something is not suitable for us, then why would we want it?

From experience, there have been a lot of things I thought would have been ideal for me; however, with time, I realized they were detrimental. Had I placed the Holy Trinity at the forefront, listening to the leading of the Spirit, I could have avoided certain predicaments I put myself through. Although God worked it out for my good, it does not justify my acts of disobedience, nor do I promote defiance.

Yes, experience is the best teacher, and *my* past mistakes have given me invaluable lessons that have shaped me into the person I am today. However, I cannot deny or downplay the pain and battle scars associated with not listening and trying to take matters into my own hands.

What is the big deal, especially when we all make mistakes? The DNA of *Win-Wins* was embedded in my genetic makeup. Yet, I willfully chose to indulge in disobedience, doing my own thing because it felt right at the time. Then again, with certain things, I did not know any better. And just because it felt right, it was NOT according to my Divine Blueprint, nor was it pleasing in the Eye of God.

As we can see, everything worked out in my favor, but I want to reiterate, 'God brought me out anyway for a time such as this.' The bottom line is that He allowed me to create *Win-Wins* out of my self-created or self-induced obstacles, only to come back to share the process of how to do likewise with such conviction that would put the enemy to boot.

So, if you have a desire to know what life has taught me about being on the *Winning Edge* and living with the threat of falling off, then let us go deeper, *As It Pleases God*.

Chapter Two

WINNING EDGE

Being on the Winning Edge is a sought-after place to be; however, the truth is, it is a Trained Mindset. Unbeknown to most, there is a *Win-Win* in all things, but we must look for *The Win-Win* for it to unveil, avail, and prevail on our behalf. If not, the human psyche will become fixed on helplessness, oppression, contamination, or defeat.

How is this possible, especially when we have it going on? Having it going on is a matter of perception. Here is what scripture has to say about being stuck in an egocentric negative demeanor, "*He has said in his heart, 'I shall not be moved; I shall never be in adversity.' His mouth is full of cursing and deceit and oppression; under his tongue is trouble and iniquity. He sits in the lurking places of the villages; in the secret places he murders the innocent; His eyes are secretly fixed on the helpless. He lies in wait secretly, as a lion in his den; he lies in wait to catch the poor; he catches the poor when he draws him into his net.*" Psalm 10:6-9. For this reason, we must retrain our mindset to become victorious amid all things while operating with the Fruits of the Spirit and Christlike Character.

As It Pleases God: Book Series

To be clear, we do not need to be the smartest or the most elite to create *Win-Wins*; all we need to do is become consistent with a Kingdomly-Trained Mindset. How will this benefit us? It helps us become Spirit-Led, putting all forms of defeat, disobedience, debauchery, and idolatry on the back burner while stepping into the LIGHT, *As It Pleases God*.

How can we determine if our LIGHT is going dim or if we are in darkness? It will vary from person to person, situation to situation, condition to condition, trauma to trauma, culture to culture, and so on. Unfortunately, the truth is that we know light from darkness, but we may be in denial. However, listed below are a few examples, but not limited to such:

- When we begin selfishly manipulating, seducing, disrespecting, or devouring others as a pastime.
- When we are confounded by the victim or the '*woe unto me*' mentality, expecting to fall short or fail.
- When we are unfaithful, unable to keep commitments, or are late all the time.
- When we are stuck feeling sorry for ourselves, moping and groping around.
- When we are constantly arguing, fussing, and fighting, we create all types of chaos.
- When we constantly complain about everything or everyone, finding nothing good to say, or outright becoming ungrateful.
- When we intentionally wound ourselves or others unnecessarily with our thoughts, actions, reactions, demeanor, words, and so on.
- When we are on an emotional rollercoaster, crying about everything, or we become so sensitive to the point where we break down quickly.
- When we become codependent on a substance to coax the psyche, pain, or trauma that is causing us to fall short, stumble, or stagger through life obliviously.
- When we begin mixing substances with other bad habits due to the lack of satisfaction.

- ☐ When we become sneaky, treacherous, and prying into the lives of others like a stalker in disguise.
- ☐ When we become a master at playing mind games to get what we want while intentionally deceiving others.

Accepting the truth can be a challenging process, especially when it conflicts with our beliefs or desires. However, it is crucial to take the time to reflect on our behaviors, thoughts, words, actions, reactions, and feelings to determine whether we are operating in a worldly mindset or a Kingdom one.

In addition, we must also take into account what or who we are dealing with as well. Here is what the Book of Proverbs wants us to know: *"My son, give me your heart, and let your eyes observe my ways. For a harlot is a deep pit, and a seductress is a narrow well. She also lies in wait as for a victim, and increases the unfaithful among men. Who has woe? Who has sorrow? Who has contentions? Who has complaints? Who has wounds without cause? Who has redness of eyes? Those who linger long at the wine, those who go in search of mixed wine. Do not look on the wine when it is red, when it sparkles in the cup, when it swirls around smoothly; at the last it bites like a serpent, and stings like a viper. Your eyes will see strange things, and your heart will utter perverse things."* Proverbs 23:26-33.

What is the purpose of knowing the above information? It preserves the human psyche from self-destructing. Plus, it helps us to build a solid foundation by knowing what will cause cracks in it. Really? Yes, really! To position ourselves on the Winning Edge, *As It Pleases God*, here is what we must know: *"Do not be envious of evil men, nor desire to be with them; for their heart devises violence, and their lips talk of troublemaking. Through wisdom a house is built, and by understanding it is established; by knowledge the rooms are filled with all precious and pleasant riches. A wise man is strong, yes, a man of knowledge increases strength; for by wise counsel, you will wage your own war, and in a multitude of counselors there is safety."* Proverbs 24:1-6.

We should never take our fruits or the fruits of others for granted. They all have meaning, and if we do not up the ante on our understanding, we will subject ourselves to becoming depleted of our positivity.

Believe it or not, negativity feeds off negligent, weak, or naive positivity, draining the life source if we do not understand how to safeguard ourselves Spiritually. Why do we need to know this? Frankly, it becomes challenging to create a *Win-Win* when we are depleted, zapped, or empty, similar to having a car running out of fuel. Listen, regardless of a vehicle's price tag, it needs some sort of fuel or electricity to get up and go. If not, it will not run properly, whereas we are the same as well.

How can we avoid this type of depletion? We need the Holy Spirit present, letting us know when to hold, fold, or walk away, ensuring we do not leave an open door to become yoked, soul-tied, burned out, or oppressed while working on ourselves from the inside out. More importantly, we need Him in the recouping process, making sure we are adequately restored according to the Will of God and not according to the will of man. Plus, when we are constantly pouring out positivity, and it is not being poured back into us, we need the Holy Spirit to intervene on our behalf, giving us the Supernatural strength to carry on in the Spirit of Excellence.

We can easily say we have it all together without the Holy Spirit; however, this is a big untruth because we are all on a learning curve with something or someone, be it known or unknown. In addition, we need the Holy Spirit, and the Holy Spirit needs us in Earthen Vessel. Closing ourselves off to the truth prolongs the learning, growing, and sowing process needed to become a master at creating *Win-Wins*. Humility in the Kingdom gets us what we need without having to toil with the human psyche and its antics.

According to the Heavenly of Heavens, when toiling with the human psyche, it means disobedience and selfishness are residing. Plus, the moment we proclaim they are NOT taking up residence from within, it only means we are not being honest with ourselves.

Who am I to judge, right? Absolutely. No judgment or pun intended, but disobedience and selfishness reside within us all. For this reason, God requires HUMILITY from us. Therefore, we must work this out of our system to ensure the Vicissitudes of Life do not break us down to the core before rebuilding us. In my opinion, some things are avoidable, and if we take heed to the Bible, especially in the Book of Proverbs, we can help ourselves stay ahead of the game when it comes down to Kingdom Protocol, *As It Pleases God*.

What other items can prevent us from creating a *Win-Win*? Our mindset determines it, be it positive or negative. The truth is, most often, when we are negative, we do not tend to realize it. We respond based upon our senses, feelings, traumas, conditioning, or obligations without knowing we must think through them positively or Kingdomly. Listed below are a few hindrances, but not limited to such:

- ☐ We do not understand '*How*' to reverse a negative into a positive to create a *Win-Win* due to some form of defeat or discouragement.
- ☐ We do not understand '*Why*' it is crucial to counteract negatives with positives, nor do we desire to hear the TRUTH, due to Spiritual Blindness, Deafness, or Muteness.
- ☐ We are too exhausted or weak Mentally, Physically, Emotionally, or Spiritually to pay attention to '*What*' we are doing to create a *Win-Win*.
- ☐ We do not have the time to approach a *Win-Win* as a form of enlightenment or deal with the transformational process.
- ☐ We are dead-set on having our way in or out of a *Win-Win* or Lose-Lose situation.
- ☐ We are offended by the *Win-Win* because it pinpoints our erring process.
- ☐ We are embarrassed to admit that the *Win-Win* will put us on blast due to some form of insecurity, causing us to lack confidence in the areas we should be excelling in.
- ☐ We are intimidated by the *Win-Win* because we do not like making mistakes or getting things wrong.

- ☐ We are not equipped to handle the *Win-Win* because we do not think we are smart or articulate enough.
- ☐ We fear the *Win-Win* will call us out of our comfort zone.
- ☐ We are not comfortable with what or who we may have to give up to achieve a *Win-Win*.
- ☐ We are confused about the process of the *Win-Win*, not knowing where to begin, or we think it is boring.

How do we position ourselves to develop a Trained Kingdom Mindset? We must learn the value of setting and achieving goals. Most often, we have a desire for everything to be instant. The instant this, instant that, putting in little or no work. Meanwhile, with a goal, it is a step-by-step process, mapping out the desired Plan of Action.

It is often said, 'Without a Plan, we plan to fail.' For the most part, this is partially true. But in the Kingdom, without failure, we lack the *Actionable Value* associated with having a Plan or the misdirection according to our Divine Blueprint. For me, I was laughed at, picked on, and judged for my failures, but it did not stop the *Win-Win* or the Plan, period.

As It Pleased God, as I became more grateful for every setback, I learned the value of creating a *Win-Win*. While at the same time, understanding the information encapsulated in the seeming failure. More importantly, I realized the only difference between my seeming failure and *Win-Win* was my PERCEPTION. Once I positively changed my perception, my Mindset transformed itself, getting me to this point for such a time as this with an epic '*Give Back!*'

As a Word to the Wise, it is imperative to pay attention to the areas of mockery, weakness, or Spiritual Attack. It is often where our Gifts, Calling, Talents, Creativity, and Purpose are hidden as stepping stones in the Eye of God. *Spirit to Spirit*, our stepping-stone lessons or training are the Spiritual Clues and Cues for *The Win-Win of Divine Greatness*. So, if we Mind Map them, they may lead us to our Divine Treasures hidden in plain sight. Then again, they may also be designed to build the Divine Cornerstone from within, *As It Pleases God.*

Once again, 'Experience is one of the best Teachers.' However, if we do not learn, understand, grow, and sow back into the Source, elevating us, we create a disservice on behalf of the Teacher. There is a Spiritual Law or Principle set in motion when we partake of a SEED. What is it? Growth and Give-Back!

For example, if we learn something, share it. If we have a meal, and someone does not have food, share. If we have something, and someone is in dire need of what we have to offer, give it to them. Blasphemy, right? Wrong. *"Give, and it will be given to you: good measure, pressed down, shaken together, and running over will be put into your bosom. For with the same measure that you use, it will be measured back to you."* Luke 6:38.

When our DNA is compromised, we will naturally feel depressed, agitated, or ambiguous, leading to all other things, feelings, or desires, regardless of whether they are good, bad, or indifferent. Yet, according to the Heavenly of Heavens, we must know and understand the difference to properly contend with what resides within.

For example, when dealing with the Spirit of Anger, a person who is in touch with themselves from the inside out can recognize the instinctual forewarning or energy relating to anger. As a result, they make the appropriate adjustments to counteract the emotion, preventing the outward expression of the lack of self-control.

On the other hand, someone who is clouded or unclear from within will not recognize anger until it begins to express itself outwardly. And then, after the fact, the individual has to play cleanup, retract actions, or repent of the ensuing actions or behaviors.

In the Kingdom, we do not want to compromise any area of our lives with the negativity of our own making or anything related to acts of disobedience. The goal is to create *Win-Wins* and not tiptoe around what will cause a losing situation predicated on our negative charactorial behaviors or patterns.

When creating *Win-Win Situations*, it is always best to stay on the positive side of the spectrum. Although we cannot control others, we can exhibit self-control, governing ourselves accordingly, even when surrounded by those willfully engaging in debauched acts. How is this possible? The *Win-Win* is being generated by and through us based on our actions, words, reactions, thoughts, beliefs, and deeds. Therefore, we are the ones who need to keep our Path of Conveyance positively clear to usher in the *Winning Spirit*.

If we desire to remain on the *Winning Edge*, we cannot worry about what everyone else is or is not doing. We can only work on ourselves to become an example for others as the *Win-Win* becomes attached to us, spreading outwardly as we become Blessed to be a Blessing.

When on the *Winning Edge*, regardless of what the vicissitudes of life have handed us, we are indeed here to help and serve according to our Divine Blueprint. To do so effectively, we need the Power of the Holy Trinity (The Father, Son, and Holy Spirit) involved. It ensures that what we are doing does not distract us from what we are Spiritually Called to do in or out of the Kingdom, or burn ourselves out.

When we are extended beyond our capacity, something or someone will suffer; therefore, we need some form of balance in all things. Yes, we want to be on the *Winning Edge*, but we must also prevent ourselves from falling off the edge. For example, all work and no play makes us dull. All winning and no rest makes us lethargic. All positives without negative counteractions to exercise our muscles make us weak and vulnerable. All Holiness without understanding or mercy makes us judgmental and condescending.

The bottom line is that when on the *Winning Edge*, we must stay in touch with reality, period. If we do not know or understand what is going on around us, our Heaven on Earth Experience suffers an imbalance. For this reason, we must harness the Power of our Seeds, ensuring we can maximize the window of time that is on our side without missing our Season of Impact.

Chapter Three

SEED POWER

As life moves on and we evolve, the power hidden in our Seeds gives birth to our *Win-Wins*, and it has enough ingenuity to prune what it does not need to thrive in its Blueprinted environment. What does this mean? When we are in our predestined environment, we will thrive by default, similar to a fish being in water, a bird having wings to fly, a lion being in the wild, and so on. Suppose we are operating in an environment contradicting our Divine Blueprint. In this case, although we have the power to adapt and make the most of the situation, it clips our wings, causing us to become limited or function at a limited capacity.

Of course, we can create a *Win-Win* out of every situation; however, the goal of this book is also to bring us into Purpose on purpose using the Gifts, Calling, Talents, and Creativity already within our DNA. What if it is not within our DNA? God gave us all something to work with! Furthermore, if we have breath in our bodies, it means we have a story (our Testimony), and that is enough to change the trajectory of our lives.

Living life to our full potential is an ideal desired status within the human psyche. For this reason, it reverts to the lust of the eye, the lust of the flesh, and the pride of life to appear better, more successful, or more whatever than we really are. In all actuality, our *Seed Power* will naturally propel us with the confidence to be who we were designed to be or do what we were called to do, *As It Pleases God*. How? We can begin using the Fruits of the Spirit and behave Christlike.

Our *Seed Power* is NOT predicated on our past, conditioning, status, or whatever is stunting our growth. The *Power* of our *Seed* is predicated on our growth from the inside out with the Fruits of the Spirit and Christlike Character. When operating against the Process of Conveyance from the Heavenly of Heavens, our negative fruits and character traits inadvertently become kryptonite. Amid living life, our kryptonite will form without us realizing what is taking place until something debilitating happens, we become traumatized to the core, or a generational curse is set in motion.

On the other hand, we also have the power to change the trajectory of our Seeds as well, but we have to want it for ourselves. Our mouths can say many things when we are desperate, but when the pressure tapers off, we often lose our enthusiasm to become better and remain as such. Therefore, God is looking for staying power, humility, and loyalty.

Listen, we must not give up or slack up for our *Seed Power* to continue building or energizing us. What is the reason to have staying power? It only takes a fraction of a second for the enemy to sift us, especially if we leave an open door justifying its entry into our lives. Therefore, we cannot give it the leverage to do so. How can we safeguard ourselves? We must Proactively Repent. How is this possible? In the same way that we can repent for a deed done. We can also Proactively Repent, avoiding any form of temptation associated with the lust of the eyes, the lust of the flesh, and the pride of life, similar to the Lord's Prayer.

If we take the time to personalize the Lord's Prayer, making it our own by applying it to our lives, we will see a difference. In my opinion, this is a great way to Repent Proactively. Besides, it keeps us from leaving ourselves open to the wiles of the enemy and protects the power hidden in our Seeds, creating a *Win-Win*. However, on the other side of the coin, if we do not know what to Repent Proactively, we need to pinpoint what is causing pain or bothering us. Once we narrow the Seed or Root of negativity, then we have what we need to reverse it into a *Positive Win-Win* without leaving it to roost or roast within us, spoiling our fruits.

Now, if we are not a professional or well-versed at pinpointing the ROOT cause or the SEEDLINGS, it is best to ask ourselves fact-finding questions and document the answers without wallowing in a bed of untruths or denial. Being we are all different, the *What, When, Where, How, Why,* and with *Whom* Formation questions work very well with this process. Listed below are a few examples, but not limited to such:

1. What is the problem or hindrance?
2. Why is it a problem or stumbling block?
3. When does this problem occur?
4. Where does this problem happen?
5. Where does this afflict us?
6. How does this problem contribute to our condition?
7. How can we reverse the effects of this problem?
8. How can we create a *Win-Win*?
9. How long do we anticipate dealing with this?
10. Who is contributing to the issue?
11. Who are we hurting or afflicting with this issue?
12. What do we plan to do about it?

In our *Q and A Sessions*, the goal is to become transparent, getting to the nitty-gritty of whatever or whomever. Plus, when we effectively communicate with ourselves, we will naturally communicate with others by default, enhancing our people skills.

According to the Heavenly of Heavens, we are designed as relational beings; therefore, it is in our nature to socialize and familiarize ourselves with the people, places, and things contributing to our cultural traditions or Bloodline, spreading abroad. What does this mean? We were designed to share who we are or our backgrounds with others from the Beginning of Time. Now, before we move on, let us align this accordingly: "*Your mother was like a vine in your bloodline, planted by the waters, fruitful and full of branches because of many waters. She had strong branches for scepters of rulers. She towered in stature above the thick branches, and was seen in her height amid the dense foliage. But she was plucked up in fury, she was cast down to the ground, and the east wind dried her fruit. Her strong branches were broken and withered; the fire consumed them. And now she is planted in the wilderness, in a dry and thirsty land. Fire has come out from a rod of her branches and devoured her fruit, so that she has no strong branch—a scepter for ruling. This is a lamentation, and has become a lamentation.*" Ezekiel 19:10-14.

For some reason, our Seeds contributing to our fruits and branches have become divided, cutting off or scattering us from those who are for us or those appearing above or beneath us. Not realizing our Kingdomly Impact does not discriminate. What does this have to do with our *Win-Wins*? It helps us to RESPECT and appreciate the differences in who we are and others without passing judgment. If we continue through life in this manner, we will lose our Spiritual Power or Impact, even if we possess worldly status, power, or influence.

Many of our issues are often rooted in a lack of appreciation, respect, or acceptance. If we can pinpoint those issues and reform them with powerful people skills, our battles will be half-won. So, what about the other half? We must engage in the *Q and A Sessions* to sort it out in our *Spirit to Spirit* Relations with the Holy Trinity. What can this do for us? When we are in direct relations with the Holy Trinity in a *Spirit to Spirit* encounter, He will usher in what and who is a part of our Blueprint and scatter those who are not. Really? Yes, really!

Here is what we need to know: "*I will bring you out from the peoples and gather you out of the countries where you are scattered, with a mighty hand, with an outstretched arm, and with fury poured out. And I will bring you into the wilderness of the peoples, and there I will plead My case with you face to face. Just as I pleaded My case with your fathers in the wilderness of the land of Egypt, so I will plead My case with you, says the Lord GOD. I will make you pass under the rod, and I will bring you into the bond of the covenant; I will purge the rebels from among you, and those who transgress against Me; I will bring them out of the country where they dwell, but they shall not enter the land of Israel. Then you will know that I am the LORD."* Ezekiel 20:34-38.

What guarantees do we have when using positive Seeds in a *Win-Win*, according to our Divine Blueprint? As a Word to the Wise, a Seed never loses its power unless it stops giving, or we stop working the Seed with Kingdom Intents or on behalf of the Kingdom. Listen, when it comes down to our Birthright or being in Purpose on purpose, God does not pull any punches.

- ☐ Either we want it, or we do not.
- ☐ We can walk into it or away from it.

According to the Heavenly of Heavens, stagnation is a surefire way to become consumed from the inside out; therefore, it behooves us to get busy converting our Seeds and Deeds into *Win-Wins* for the Kingdom. How do we make our Seeds create a *Win-Win*? Listed below are a few tips, but not limited to such:

- ☐ In the *Win-Win*, we must be willing to learn, expanding ourselves from worldly to Kingdomly.

- ☐ In the *Win-Win*, we must be willing to grow, avoiding the cycle of déjà vu or stagnation.

- ☐ In the *Win-Win*, we must be willing to sow, giving back to the system of conveyance, while causing the Law of Reciprocity or Seedtime and Harvest to favor us consistently, or anyone and anything connected to us as well.

- ☐ In the *Win-Win*, we must be willing to build, bridging the negative gaps into positive seals.

- ☐ In the *Win-Win*, we must be willing to Spiritually Till our own ground and put in the necessary work from the inside out.

- ☐ In the *Win-Win*, we must be willing to think positively, leaving no stone unturned, while becoming better daily and a consistent work-in-progress toward Greatness.

- ☐ In the *Win-Win*, we must be willing to redo, renew, regraft, or revamp.

- ☐ In the *Win-Win*, we must be willing to become equipped with the Spiritual Tools needed to thrive with a Positive Mental Attitude amid negativity or worldliness.

- ☐ In the *Win-Win*, we must be willing to become totally committed to the Kingdom without deviation or second-guessing ourselves. At the same time, becoming flexible to stand in the gap when necessary or when called upon.

- ☐ In the *Win-Win*, we must be willing to forgive, offer compassion, have mercy, and become thankful for all things, including the good, bad, and ugly.

- ☐ In the *Win-Win*, we must be willing to put away jealousy, envy, pride, coveting, hatefulness, competitiveness, disrespectfulness, disobedience, greed, or any form of debauchery.

- ☐ In the *Win-Win*, we must be willing to use the Fruits of the Spirit and exhibit Christlike Character in all things, regardless of the dream killers or naysayers.

The bottom line is that in the *Win-Win*, we are active participants in this process, regardless of the expectations set before us by others. In the Kingdom, we are the contributing force to how we think, what we feel, what affects us, where it is taking place, or why we are dealing with whatever or whomever.

In the Eye of God, we are responsible for ourselves, regardless of the situation, circumstance, or position we find ourselves in, even if it is not our fault. In addition, it helps us to get rid of laying the blame elsewhere while developing our mindsets and perspectives, positively or negatively. But for the sake of this book, we will keep this on the positive side of the spectrum, ensuring the *Win-Win* is obtained and sustained in our *Spirit to Spirit* Connection to the Heavenly of Heavens.

What does our *Spirit to Spirit* Connection have to do with assuming responsibility? Irresponsibility in the Kingdom is a big no-no. We have innocent people involved in the nurturing, learning, growing, and commissioning process; therefore, we cannot exhibit recklessness, causing someone to get caught up with a one-way ticket into the Pit. If it happens and is left unrepentant, we are accountable. Is this fair? Absolutely, especially if we are knowingly behaving like a wolf in sheep's clothing. Or, if we are not using the Fruits of the Spirit, our character is negatively flawed without attempting to put in the work from the inside out, or we have totally ignored the leading of the Holy Spirit to do our own thing.

Clearly, I am not condemning anyone to the Pit. Still, in the Kingdom, we do not get a free pass to do whatever we like, with whomever, and not give an account, especially when the Spirit of Love is nowhere in the equation. Yet, let us align, "*They will give an account to Him who is ready to judge the living and the dead. For this reason, the gospel was preached also to those who are dead, that they might be judged according to men in the flesh, but live according to God in the Spirit. But the end of all things is at hand; therefore, be serious and watchful in your prayers. And above all things have fervent love for one another, for 'love will cover a multitude of sins.'*" 1 Peter 4:5-8.

As God Promised, genuine love and respect go a long way in any given situation, primarily when we use the Fruits of the Spirit and Christlike Character to water our Seeds and Deeds in or out of the Kingdom. As we all know, the absence of love is hate. So it is fair to say that if we are not operating in the Spirit of Love, hate is blocking the transfer of genuine Spiritual Righteousness.

How is this possible when we are doing the right things and treating people right? Just because we exercise self-control in certain areas or with certain people, it does not mean we are exhibiting righteous behaviors according to Kingdom Standards or the Fruits of the Spirit. We must take a look at the Seeds and Deeds hidden in the manifestations of our fruits. Why do we need to examine ourselves in such a manner? For example, but not limited to such:

- ☐ A hateful person is not going to admit outright that they are hateful or that their behaviors exhibit hatefulness.

- ☐ A nice person in public will not openly admit they go home to a toxic environment, cussing out everyone, including the dog. They have an image to keep, and they are not going to risk being put on blast. So, what do they do? They put on a nice mask and keep it moving.

- ☐ A rude person will not admit they are leaving a trail of traumatized victims or behaving rudely. Most often, the rudest individuals think they are really helping someone. But, based upon their conditioning, understanding, or biases, they lack the people skills or the Spiritual Etiquette to kindly convey information without rubbing people the wrong way.

- ☐ A happy person in public will not admit they are wallowing in a bed of hurt, discouragement, and rejection. So, what do they do? They cover it up by masking their discontentment with lusts, habits, gossip, lies, activities, work, addictions, pompousness, and so on, without pinpointing the Root or Seed of whatever they are facing from within.

- ☐ A jealous or envious person will not admit they are coveting or comparing themselves with everyone they come in contact with.

- ☐ A person appearing on the *Winning Edge* in public will not admit they are battling with competitiveness. So, what do they do? They mask their desires to throw someone under the bus or betray them when the opportunity presents itself for them to take the lead.

- ☐ An evil person is not going to openly admit they thrive on debauchery, chaos, and confusion.

- ☐ A seemingly patient person in public will not admit they are a slave driver or control freak behind closed doors. So, what do they do? Once again, they mask it.

- ☐ A selfish person will not admit to being openly selfish or exhibiting selfish behaviors.

- ☐ A sell-out will not admit that they are not to be trusted.

- ☐ A person driven by cursing others will not admit that we will become their victim if we get their timing wrong.

- ☐ A lazy, unapologetic, or angry employee will not admit that they will make a business suffer their wrath, causing them to lose customers inadvertently.

In the Spirit of Excellence, regardless of whether the Seed is planted in our personal or professional lives, it will take ROOT, positively or negatively. So, beware. We would be surprised at how many businesses are suffering or losing business due to negative, lackadaisical employees.

Although we cannot control everyone, we can control the Seeds of Service. How? If an employee receives wages, they fall under the Company's Vision to receive the agreed-upon provisions. Now, if their Seeds of Service are affecting the bottom line negatively, or if they are traumatizing customers, it is our responsibility to draw the line in the sand, period!

Many companies have become a little lax about quality service and retaining customers; however, be reminded that there are Spiritual Laws governing how individuals are treated. The pop-up shops are all over the place, and corporations are making their mark; yet, it changes the rules of the Spiritual Clout covering the entity when we operate without integrity.

The *Win-Win of Divine Greatness* is available in every situation and with anyone. Whether we are setting the stage for ourselves, our family, or our company, we are accountable for leading our field with outright integrity with the Fruits of the Spirit and Christlike Character, *As It Pleases God*. For this reason, we must pay attention to our thoughts, words, actions, behaviors, demeanor, and so on, LEADING BY EXAMPLE.

Chapter Four

SITUATIONAL *WIN-WINS*

Situational *Win-Wins* are just as important as conventional ones. As life would have it, some *Win-Wins* are predictable; for example, if something bad happens, we look for the good. If we get angry, we must find something to become happy about. Meanwhile, a *Situational Win-Win* is unpredictably in action, where nothing is set in stone; therefore, we have to go with the flow or outright break the flow. For this reason, we must build our proactive skills, *As It Pleases God*, enabling us to think on our feet at the drop of a dime.

Approaching a *Situational Win-Win* is indeed a hands-on approach, allowing us to get involved in the equation with practical and applied strategies. Applicatorily, we have free will to invite the Holy Trinity into this approach, but we must choose to win on our own terms (without God) or that of the Kingdom (with God).

In or out of the Kingdom, these Spiritual Principles work, even if we are Non-Believers. Nevertheless, the level of Divine Intervention is predicated on the Holy Trinity being involved in the *Situational Win-Win*. What does this mean? If we desire

Spiritual Help, we must connect to the Spiritual Means of receiving it. Simply put, we must SET the Atmosphere, *As It Pleases God*. Without Him or when pleasing ourselves, we are limited in the Realm of the Spirit. Listed below are a few examples, but not limited to such:

- ☐ In a *Win-Win* situation, we must be able to think on or off our feet, especially when challenged or our inner qualities are in question by those seeking to discredit what they do not understand. For this reason, it is always best to develop our people skills, ensuring we can relate to others on any level and under any circumstances.

- ☐ In a *Win-Win* situation, we must become readily available to the Will of God, our Divine Blueprint, or step into Purpose on purpose. When in the Kingdom, we are on call 24/7. Frankly, those who are faithful, proactive, obedient, and dependable are usually the ones who are rationed out more Gifts of the Spirit than those who are wishy-washy, unpredictable, and unreliable. Some would call this favoritism, but in the Kingdom, we call this being in Purpose on purpose, doing what it takes to get the job done.

- ☐ In a *Win-Win* situation, we become proactively helpful without judging another man's condition. We do not know what God is doing or how He is training someone unless the Holy Spirit reveals it; therefore, it is best to approach everyone as if they are already in a Spiritual Classroom.

- ☐ In a *Win-Win* situation, it is best to make the lives of others easier, if possible. How do we go about doing so? By empowering them with the Spiritual Information, Tools, or Know-How to move to the next level. If we dare to withhold information, especially when it is within our power to release it, we become limited in the Kingdom. The Divine Well of Wisdom does not discriminate, nor does it withhold information because of a superficial price tag.

In the Kingdom, the goal is to save lives by any means necessary. In my opinion, every CHANCE is a fighting one; therefore, we should never deprive anyone of this opportunity. If we do, we will find our well running dry, especially when it should be overflowing with the people, places, and things money cannot buy.

- [ ] In a *Win-Win* situation, we must approach any situation as a giver and not a taker. We are Blessed to be a Blessing, and when we approach life with this Positive Mental Mindset, our cup or portion will runneth over.

- [ ] In a *Win-Win* situation, we must plan for success by documenting, strategizing, and Mind Mapping.

- [ ] In a *Win-Win* situation, we must begin to manage our time properly. If we are busy running around doing and achieving nothing, then it is best to reevaluate the time spent.

- [ ] In a *Win-Win* situation, we must build our *Spirit to Spirit* Relations with prayer, repentance, fasting on occasion, and meditating on the Word of God.

- [ ] In a *Win-Win* situation, we must begin to use positive affirmations to replace the negative chatter. We are often taught to cast down negativity, but we are not taught to replace it with positivity. By doing so, it establishes consistency instead of inconsistent gaps.

- [ ] In a *Win-Win* situation, we must avoid procrastination. It ruins our credibility.

- [ ] In a *Win-Win* situation, we must not have a problem with delegating when necessary.

- [ ] In a *Win-Win* situation, we must focus amid distractions designed to sift us, Mentally, Physically, Emotionally, or Spiritually.

If we dare to unpack the world's way of winning to embrace the Kingdom's way of creating a *Win-Win*, there is no limit to what we can achieve, *As It Pleases God*.

Unbeknown to most, in the *Win-Win*, the fight is already fixed. All we need to do is search for it with clean hands and a pure heart, along with the desire to receive the Blessing to become a Blessing. Why are we not able to enjoy our own Blessings without sharing? Selfish Blessings are fleeting ones, or they may feel like a curse due to the yoke placed on them. Who places the yoke? We place the yoke by becoming selfish, stingy, or self-centered.

If we desire to place a Spiritual Seal on any form of *Win-Win* or Blessing, we must activate the Law of Reciprocity. Once we break the flow of Blessings, we inadvertently create dams or blockages from the inside out.

To be clear, this does not mean squandering our Blessings. We must become good stewards and incorporate Divine Wisdom in this process. According to the Heavenly of Heavens, here is what we must know: "*There is desirable treasure, and oil in the dwelling of the wise, but a foolish man squanders it. He who follows righteousness and mercy finds life, righteousness and honor.*" Proverbs 21:20-21.

Once we rise to the occasion to create *Situational Win-Wins*, we can make it easier for ourselves or create difficulty. For me, I will automatically choose to take a positive way, benefiting the Kingdom. By doing so, I keep my hands BLESSED, knowing whatever I touch or become involved in will experience an overflow. How is this possible? I use Spiritual Principles and Fruits, *As It Pleases God*.

More importantly, I activate the Law of Reciprocity with Spiritual Seals in scriptures such as: *"As each one has received a gift, minister it to one another, as good stewards of the manifold grace of God."* 1 Peter 4:10. For this reason, my EXPECTATIONS are always of Divine Favor, Blessings, Wisdom, and Overflow; therefore, my FAITH is not easily shaken because whatever I need, I GIVE it!

In my *Spirit to Spirit* Communal sessions with my Heavenly Father, here is how I Spiritually Seal my Birthright Blessings with Spiritual Decrees:

- ☐ I arise to RAISE another.
- ☐ Show me the love I can freely SHARE with others.
- ☐ Speak through me to IMPART life to another.
- ☐ Bless me to BLESS others.
- ☐ Strengthen me to STRENGTHEN another.
- ☐ Heal me to HEAL others.
- ☐ Tend to my needs so I can FEED Your sheep.
- ☐ Grant me Wisdom to IMPART Wisdom to others.
- ☐ Release Divine Provisions to PROVIDE Provisions.
- ☐ Anoint my Spiritual Fruits so I can SHARE the Fruits of the Spirit with others.
- ☐ Polish my Character Traits to ensure I am SHARING Christlike Characteristics and impeccable people skills.
- ☐ As my cup runneth over, allow it to OVERFLOW into the lives of others.

As God Promised, regardless of where we are in life, we will always have something to share, even if we are on our last leg, Mentally, Physically, Emotionally, or Spiritually. Amid all, we should never approach life with an empty hand. It behooves us to give in the area of our need, pain, or greed. Unbeknown to most, it helps to polish our Creativity in creating *Win-Win Situations,* and it breaks the Spirit of Lack.

Plus, our Gifts, Calling, and Talents are often hidden in the Creativity invoked in our area of giving out of the illusion of lack. How is this possible to give when we lack? We must find a way to become Creative; it reverses a negative mindset, letting us know we have it. We simply need to find it, make arrangements, or manifest it. Listed below are a few examples, but not limited to such:

- ☐ If we need respect, give it.
- ☐ If we need provision, give it.
- ☐ If we need love, give it.
- ☐ If we need attention, give it.
- ☐ If we need understanding, give it.
- ☐ If we need support, give it.
- ☐ If we need a Blessing, give it.
- ☐ If we need a relationship, give it.
- ☐ If we need hope, give it.
- ☐ If we need forgiveness, give it.
- ☐ If we need mercy, give it.
- ☐ If we need peace, give it.

These reciprocal concepts have been around since the Ancient of Days. Yet, in our present-day situations, we have forgotten. How is it possible to forget this? Conditioning and adaptation will do it to us every time, primarily when we do not involve God in our equational efforts. What is the big deal? It creates a selfish mindset.

For example, from a child's perspective, they do not know anything about being impoverished unless taught or conditioned into this mindset. If we do not condition their mind in such a manner, they will play, create, and have fun, creating toys out of the natural elements of nature. While at the same time making friends with anyone, practicing their newfound independence without any form of bias whatsoever.

From experience, this is really where our Creativity is generated for our adult years. If a child's Creativity is stunted, they will become limited in making something out of nothing while expecting everything to be ready-made or instant. Plus, there are times it will stunt their ability to deal with certain types of situations, circumstances, and events.

Unfortunately, the mind can become conditionally locked, especially if we are not trained to understand and question ourselves, people, places, and things accordingly. For example, we now have smartphones, and the children of today's day and age come with an intuitive knowledge of how to use them without being taught. Yet, they do not know about a rotary phone or how to use it unless they are taught.

Can we really become creative as children? Of course. Believe it or not, our Creativity is at its best when we are children. For me, my Creativity began with sticks, stones, trees, and junk. It was nothing fancy, but it served its Divine Purpose.

Back in the day, most laughed at me for playing with things they presumed to be repulsive or dirty. But, in my little mind at the time, I was Blessed to have a smorgasbord of things to play with to create something new every single day. More importantly, I did not mind getting my hands dirty while doing so. Actually, I had a blast!

Here is the deal: At five years old, I learned how to take what people took for granted or threw away to create something beautiful in my eyes. This childhood experience that my Grandmother ushered in through an act of nurturing and training conditioned me for a time such as this.

What do sticks, stones, trees, and junk have to do with our *Win-Win*? It took the limits off my mind to envision what most cannot see, accomplish what most cannot, endure what would break the average person, and build what most would tear down. As a result, I learned how to create *Win-Win Situations* since the age of five. So, I am well-versed in the information the Heavenly of Heavens are allowing me to share. Had my Grandmother prevented me from experiencing that moment in time, I would not be here, sharing this profound information. Even though I did not know about my Divine Blueprint or Destined Path, my Grandmother knew.

How did she know? First and foremost, she was a Spiritual Woman of God, and she named me. Secondly, she knew it was her responsibility to plant the SEEDS at an early age, that I would need to sustain the Spiritual Fruits of my Spiritual Journey. Thirdly, she knew in due time that God would call me to reach out to help others create *Win-Wins* out of things other people take for granted.

In or out of the Vicissitudes of Life, I take nothing for granted. Why? First, it provides me with an opportunity to humbly heed to the Gifts, Calling, Talents, and Creativity set forth by the Heavenly of Heavens. Secondly, it assists me in searching for the *Win-Win*, especially when others see loss or defeat. Thirdly, it guides me in searching for the NEST EGG of Divine Wisdom. Yes, the same Wisdom nesting from the Ancient of Days until NOW, which is ready to come home to roost, doing what it has been destined to do from the Beginning.

We can take life for a joke if we like. But in the end, it will not be a laughing matter when the joke is on us. Why would the joke be on us? For not taking heed to how to reverse the negative into a positive, wrong to right, unjust to just, unrighteousness to righteousness, evil to good, and so on.

In my opinion, it is appalling when our children have to deal with or put an end to the issues we refuse to face. Is this fair? Absolutely not. It is our responsibility to teach and prepare them on how to deal with the Vicissitudes of Life, not how to avoid, ignore, downplay, whitewash, or make them think they are better than life itself. Had my Grandmother protected me from the Creative Forces and Divine Lessons hidden in the sticks, stones, trees, and junk, one would not be reading this book right now. Nor would I be able to break the bones of negativity to create a *Win-Win*, regardless.

I am forever grateful for the natural elements of life and for God allowing my Grandmother to usher me into the greatest asset known to man. What is the greatest asset? It is the connection back to NATURE itself.

The natural elements of life can spark the unearthed rudiments of the human psyche that science has not discovered yet. How is this possible? We are in Earthen Vessels. Simply put, we are

Vessels of God, and no one will have all the details to outdo the Creator or His Divine Words. Is this Biblical? I would have it no other way. *"Heaven and earth will pass away, but My words will by no means pass away. But of that day and hour no one knows, not even the angels of heaven, but My Father only."* Matthew 24:35-36.

Some would say this scripture is not applicable; however, I beg to differ! So, my question is, 'What is He returning to?' My point exactly: EARTH! We are in Earthen Vessels, even if we do not know that we are. Please allow me to Spiritually Align, *As It Pleases God*. *"But we have this treasure in earthen vessels, that the excellence of the power may be of God and not of us."* 2 Corinthians 4:7.

If we dare to take advantage of the natural, yet intangible Blessings in plain sight, it will revolutionize our lives in ways that would trump human reasoning on any day of the week. Listen, if one has not noticed by now, when referring to or talking about the human psyche, it is also predicated on our human nature. How is it that nature is a part of our humanness, providing a direct connection to man's psyche? Yet, we fail to understand it.

The interconnection of nature and our psyche is indeed connected to life, and if we do not understand this, we will find ourselves tripping out when we should be tripping forward into the Arms of the Kingdom. Whatever we consider a luxury is formed from some element of nature, and we have the nerve to become ungrateful. For this reason, Mother Nature has no mercy on those interfering with the natural contexture of seasons, nor disrespecting that which is DIVINE.

Chapter Five

TRIP SWITCH

We often hear about someone tripping out, or we may find ourselves tripping out from time to time. Yet, we do not usually take the time to understand the underlying reason causing such behavior. The reason could be hidden in our lack of self-control, conditioning, understanding, culture, biases, and so on. However, we do not know another man's story unless we take the time to ask the right fact-finding questions or get a complete understanding to better create a *Win-Win*.

Even if the *Win-Win* is rejected, we are required to do our part in exhibiting the Fruits of the Spirit and Christlike Character, fixing our Spiritual Crown first and then helping others. Why must we work on ourselves first? It keeps our countenance from falling, especially when our approach to the *Win-Win* is rejected.

When searching for the *Win-Win* in all things, regardless of how it appears, it helps avoid placing false expectations or becoming susceptible to failed ones. How does this work? If we train the mind to search for the *Win-Win*, we take the disappointment out of the equation, and we become less provoked by not having things go the way we anticipated.

Unbeknown to most, in order to have a *Win-Win*, we need a TRIGGER, be it positive or negative. It is indeed the SEED provoking our awareness or demanding our attention. Now, how we respond depends firstly upon our MINDSET and then our conditioning, biases, and so on. In so many words, it is a Trip Switch to a *Positive Win-Win* or a negative lose-lose. We must understand ourselves from the inside out to properly govern the Seedful Triggers. Here is why, but not limited to such:

- ☐ A Triggered thought means something.
- ☐ A Triggered emotion means something.
- ☐ A Triggered word means something.
- ☐ A Triggered event means something.
- ☐ A Triggered reaction means something.
- ☐ A Triggered precept means something.
- ☐ A Triggered reason means something.
- ☐ A Triggered perception means something.
- ☐ A Triggered instinct means something.
- ☐ A Triggered conscience means something.
- ☐ Triggered writing means something.
- ☐ A Triggered whatever has something to unveil, reveal, detail, or prune.

What that SOMETHING is, is indeed up to us! Why is this left up to us? If we are not ready to receive it, we will not get it, no matter how hard we try. Where do Triggers come from? They can come from anything or anyone; they do not discriminate. Yet, if we fail to understand or listen, we become Spiritually Blind, Deaf, and Mute to the Triggers.

In today's day and age, there are certain Triggers designed to destroy the hope residing in the human psyche. For example, we have someone who is asked about their Spiritual Passion or Purpose. When they open up to share, the person who asked the question continues to interject negativity or some form of pain to distract the person when speaking. By far, this happens all too often, usually leading to frustration, but we must recognize it for what it is...a Triggered Distraction. Clearly, this does not make the person bad; it is the behavior that needs to be dealt with. So, be careful when dealing with such behavior to ensure it does not provoke an adverse reaction from within, causing us to lash out.

On the other hand, Positive Triggers are extremely powerful if we learn how to use or reverse any negative situation into a positive *Win-Win*. For example, the way I have been Spiritually Anointed and Ordained to write, *As It Pleases God*, it must Spiritually Trigger something from within the human psyche, provoking an element of thought, emotion, feeling, questioning, reasoning, quickening, or something. What is the purpose of this? It provides a connection to the Written Words streamed from the Heavenly of Heavens or the Power of my Testament or Testimony. How is this possible? Simply put, I use Triggers to create *Win-Wins* with a Positive Mental Mindset as my '*Take Away*,' with the intent to '*Give Back*' to the Divine Source freely giving to me.

To take this a step further, in the Spirit of Righteousness, I empower Triggers with a Spiritual Seal, using Kingdom Perspectives and Spiritual Principles to create evolutionary balance from the Ancient of Days to NOW. What does this mean? I use the Word of God to align Triggers with Biblical Truths, the Fruits of the Spirit, and Christlike Character. Once done, I then share my findings to help and empower others to do likewise.

To be clear, the Spiritual Classroom and my Evolutionary Transformation ordained by the Heavenly of Heavens was not an overnight process. I have been in Spiritual Training for years for such a time as this. Nevertheless, for others, the turnaround time from this point forward will be much shorter due to the Unveiled Instructions at our fingertips.

Now, regardless of where we are in the Spiritual Revamping Process, it is always best to proactively prepare ourselves when people, places, and things have the potential to go to the left. For this reason, when things do not go our way, here are a few things to do, but not limited to such:

- ☐ We can usher in the Holy Spirit for assistance.
- ☐ We can cover our Mind, Body, Soul, and Spirit with the Blood of Jesus.
- ☐ We can become instantly grateful. Giving thanks for all things helps us appreciate all aspects of life.
- ☐ We can invoke peace and relaxation.
- ☐ We can pray.
- ☐ We can forgive and repent.
- ☐ We can interject scriptures.
- ☐ We can reaffirm with positive affirmations.
- ☐ We can realign our thoughts and document our findings.
- ☐ We can adjust how we feel, aligning them with the Fruits of the Spirit.
- ☐ We can allow the autonomy of free will.
- ☐ We can look for a way to proactively help someone else while exhibiting Christlike Character.

Will this really work for us? Absolutely. Now, the key to making this work on our behalf is to remain CALM. Really? Yes, really! To rationally create *Win-Wins*, we must exhibit self-control, Mentally, Physically, Emotionally, and Spiritually.

So, when others are busy reacting, we are busy peacefully thinking, calculating, positioning, strategizing, aligning, and so on, creating a formula for the *Win-Win*. Plus, if we add the Holy Spirit into this equation, we will become a force to be reckoned with in a mighty way. Listed below are a few 'Need to Know' when positioning ourselves for the *Win-Win*, but not limited to such:

- ☐ We need truth and transparency in, out, or amid the search for the *Win-Win*.

- ☐ We must pride ourselves in learning more to get to the *Win-Win*, while clearing our Mental Portal or Cobwebs to receive new, articulate, profound, or strategic information.

As It Pleases God: Book Series

- ☐ We must understand the benefits associated with the *Win-Win* while giving thanks in all things, even if it does not appear as such to the naked eye.

- ☐ We must show interest in the *Win-Win*. When we are attentive to the *Win-Win*, it avails itself in ways to trump human reasoning, letting us know that it is present, active, and calculative.

- ☐ We must be willing to inspire ourselves and others in the *Win-Win*. If we dare to want more *Win-Win Situations* in our lives, we should give them to others to create an overflow. For example, the more I share positive information according to my Divine Blueprint from the Ancient of Ancients, the more it overflows, continuing to express itself in uncommon ways, superseding human logic.

- ☐ We must be able to apply the *Win-Win*, causing all things to work together for our good. In the Beginning of the Book of Genesis, God said all things were GOOD. Notably, this means that they still are; however, we must Spiritually Till the good out of whatever or whomever from the inside out.

- ☐ We must be able to produce the evidence of our *Win-Wins* through the power of our Testimony, living by example, and showing others how to do likewise, going from a *'hearer'* to a *'doer'* positively.

- ☐ We must be willing to use our Gifts, Talents, Calling, Purpose, and Creativity in the formulation of the *Win-Win*.

- ☐ We must be willing to think inside, outside, around, through, over, and under the box, leaving no stone unturned to obtain the *Win-Win* in a state of peace, harmony, and balance.

☐ We must put away overthinking or overdoing it, while using consistency, positivity, and confidence in the *Win-Win*, giving us the ability to put people, places, and things in their proper perspective or according to Divine Order.

☐ We must nurture our *Win-Win Situations* with positive affirmations. They are connected to us; therefore, they can effectively RELATE.

☐ We must communicate with our *Win-Wins*, causing them to reciprocate with the strategies, know-how, mysteries, and secrets of the *Win-Win*.

Who knows the *Win-Win* better than the *Win-Win*? Of course, God knows the *Win-Win*, but the *Win-Win* and the Holy Spirit have the Spiritual Details or Blueprint, and the Blood of Jesus has the Spiritual Covering needed, permitting us to possess what belongs to us rightfully. The bottom line is that the package deal of our *Win-Win* is Divinely Linked to the Holy Trinity.

To be clear, we can obtain *Win-Wins* without the Holy Spirit with a Positive Mental Mindset; however, it becomes hit or miss based on our condition. If our Divine Blueprint is not involved, we are limited in the orchestration of what is Kingdom, while still usable outside of Kingdom Formality. What does this mean? We still have access to Spiritual Principles and practical information through reading or educating ourselves. Yet, we are limited in the execution of them until the proper conditions or prerequisites are met, *As It Pleases God*.

For example, when we visit the mall, we have legal access to every store. Still, we cannot take possession of what is in the store until the proper conditions are met. In other words, if we are not able to pay for what we want, we cannot gain access to the merchandise. Moreover, if we gain illegal access, there is an even higher penalty associated.

Now, as we bring this back into our reality, it is best to arm ourselves with the Spiritual Principles from the Heavenly of Heavens. To ensure we are on the right track and downloading the correct information from the accurate Source, governing our *Righteous Win-Wins*.

The Building Blocks of Spirituality, according to the Heavenly of Heavens, are available to all. Why do we need Building Blocks? One action, behavior, thought, and so on is built upon another, positively or negatively. If we are clueless or simply going with the flow, we can become easily or negatively TRIGGERED. Therefore, using Spiritual Building Blocks helps keep us from becoming victims of the negative *Trip Switches* designed to derail us. For this reason, in the building process, we must know how to place one block upon another positively.

Why can we not simply build with whatever and whomever? We should exercise extreme caution when putting a positive block on a negative one and vice versa. Mixing our building blocks in any manner without Spiritual Discretion can create an implosion or explosion, especially when the conditions are right or the Trigger is set accordingly.

Of course, we will all have our moments, but we should never position ourselves to allow our moments to have us. We must equip ourselves to bounce back, dealing with whatever or whomever quickly as if nothing happened, fully functioning with a Kingdom Mindset. Is this humanly possible? Of course, it is.

If we deal with Building Blocks instead of everything all in one, we can better use a step-by-step process in adding or eliminating, doing and redoing, grafting and regrafting, and so on. For example, we will never see a building erected at once. It is a process of setting the necessary underground network of piping, connecting the outlets for waste, setting the foundation for stability, erecting the walls for protection, placing the roof for covering, installing windows and doors for an opening or connection to the outside world, connecting the connection of electrical wiring giving us the accessible power to live comfortably, and so on.

If we run into a problem with the electrical wiring, we do not have to rebuild the house. We can deal with the wiring without touching the plumbing because they are unrelated and have nothing to do with each other.

Suppose we use Spiritual Building Blocks or Spiritual Principles in such a manner. In this case, we can deal with the one issue without having a compilation of negative issues piggybacking on our positivity or ruining us. But do not take my word for it; let us take this to scripture: *"Whoever comes to Me, and hears My sayings and does them, I will show you whom he is like: He is like a man building a house, who dug deep and laid the foundation on the rock. And when the flood arose, the stream beat vehemently against that house, and could not shake it, for it was founded on the rock. But he who heard and did nothing is like a man who built a house on the earth without a foundation, against which the stream beat vehemently; and immediately it fell. And the ruin of that house was great."* Luke 6:47-49.

Regardless of where we are, what we have been through, or how we feel about God, *Spiritual Principles* help with the Spiritual Etiquette needed to abase and abound amid getting ourselves together. Here is the scripture to hold close to the heart when creating a *Win-Win* on any level, *"Not that I speak in regard to need, for I have learned in whatever state I am, to be content: I know how to be abased, and I know how to abound. Everywhere and in all things I have learned both to be full and to be hungry, both to abound and to suffer need. I can do all things through Christ who strengthens me."* Philippians 4:11-13. With this knowledge and repeating, '*I can do all things through Christ who strengthens me*' when planning, documenting, or seeking the *Win-Win*, I promise it will begin to change the trajectory of anyone's life. I am living proof with no shame attached!

The '*No Shame Attached*' dynamics are wrapped in the Divine Secrets of how to prepare ourselves for our Heaven on Earth Experience. Frankly, no one likes to be put to shame, even if we are an expert *Win-Win* creator; therefore, to avoid this deceptional trick from happening within the human psyche, we must question our fruits, creating a Wisdom Notch instead of a thorn in our flesh. Most thorns are self-created, and GOD ALLOWED.

With the above promise, if we target the Seed or our *Trip Switch* and then align it with the Fruits of the Spirit, we will be better able to understand what we should or should not have done. How? We must begin to document, document, document, keeping a running list of our provocations and how we plan to realign ourselves using the Fruits of the Spirit. Now, when using the charts to do so, we must do two things:

- ☐ We must state the issue, action, or behavior, and then answer the question of whether or not a specific Spiritual Fruit was used by checking the appropriate box.

- ☐ We must list the proposed solution and then ask again if the Spiritual Fruits are being exhibited in the solution. If the answer is 'No,' we must rewrite a better solution.

Fruits of the Spirit	What is the Issue, Action, or Behavior?	Is it exhibiting ___ ?
1. Love.		Yes ☐ or No ☐
2. Joy.		Yes ☐ or No ☐
3. Peace.		Yes ☐ or No ☐
4. Patience.		Yes ☐ or No ☐
5. Kindness.		Yes ☐ or No ☐
6. Goodness.		Yes ☐ or No ☐
7. Faithfulness.		Yes ☐ or No ☐
8. Gentleness.		Yes ☐ or No ☐
9. Self-Control.		Yes ☐ or No ☐

Fruits of the Spirit	What is the proposed solution?	Is it exhibiting ___ ?
1. Love.		Yes ☐ or No ☐
2. Joy.		Yes ☐ or No ☐
3. Peace.		Yes ☐ or No ☐
4. Patience.		Yes ☐ or No ☐
5. Kindness.		Yes ☐ or No ☐
6. Goodness.		Yes ☐ or No ☐
7. Faithfulness.		Yes ☐ or No ☐
8. Gentleness.		Yes ☐ or No ☐
9. Self-Control.		Yes ☐ or No ☐

According to the Heavenly of Heavens, whether we know how to create a *Win-Win* or not, most of us want to capitalize on opportunities without having to work, use the Fruits of the Spirit, or exhibit Christlike Character as our Seeds of Conveyance. However, we must know according to Psalm 22:30: *"A seed shall serve him; it shall be accounted to the Lord for a generation."* Thus, the positive or negative Seeds we are planting or squandering today will pass down to our Bloodline.

In the *Win-Win*, if we are inadvertently dealing with unfruitful or negative Seeds, we have the opportunity to regraft, uproot, or circumvent the Seed. But there is a catch! We must adequately redirect the trajectory of a Seed into a worthy *Win-Win*, and we must understand the 'Why' of it as well. The 'Why' will vary from person to person, but the self-analysis process does not, nor should we compare ourselves with others when doing so. We must compare ourselves to ourselves by the analysis of our fruits and character traits. If we indulge in comparing, we will end up with the wrong results every time. We all have a different Predestined Blueprint; therefore, the Seed embedded into the human psyche will not be the same, especially for deep-rooted issues.

According to the Heavenly of Heavens, for surface issues, dealing with our senses is not such a big deal when using a pre-planned method of bringing about a resolution. For example, if we smell donuts, and it is not a donut we are smelling, it is a cake; all we need to do is correct our perception, and our smell will adjust itself to perceive a cake smell. However, when it comes down to anything dealing with the lust of the eyes, the lust of the flesh, and the pride of life, it is not as simple. It is indeed a Spiritual Matter, even if we attempt to play pretend or band-aid the issues. Simply put, something means something when we are Triggered positively or negatively. So, when our *Trip Switch* is set off, if we learn how to MASTER creating *Win-Wins*, we can respond appropriately with the Fruits of the Spirit, Christlike Character, and Spiritual Principles, even if it is not such a pleasant Trigger.

Chapter Six

SPIRITUAL PRINCIPLES

The Spiritual Principles governing our *Win-Win* are not as difficult as one would think. Once again, the *Win-Win* is a part of our DNA, and if we dare to look within to learn, understand, and grow, we will never do without. How is this humanly possible? Doing without is a MINDSET, and if we revamp ourselves to possess a Kingdom Mindset, there is no lack. There are only Lessons, Blessings, Revelations, and Tests redirecting us to the *Win-Win*, a State of Obedience, or our Divine Destiny.

Here is the deal: Most of us stop at practical information, not tapping into the Spiritual Aspects of our being. As a result, we appear as if we are on the *Win-Win*, but from within, we feel as if we are losing ground. But today, I am here to say, 'It is NORMAL.' Actually, it is a RED FLAG from the Realm of the Spirit, letting us know that there is an imbalance somewhere or with someone.

On the other hand, what is NOT normal is to remain in this condition without Spiritual Intervention. Our Spiritual DNA is calling us out of worldliness into a Kingdom Mindset; therefore, the human psyche will struggle for control, keeping us locked in on or distracted by the lust of the eyes, the lust of the flesh, and the pride of life. Spiritually Speaking, we have the power to reverse the effects taking place from within by becoming a positive work-in-progress.

When we can consistently work on ourselves from the inside out while maintaining our focus, we can spot the little quirks causing the mind to jump the track or what is causing a disturbance from within. We can tiptoe around what we feel, but the truth is that it relates to something, and if we do not understand what that something is or is not, we create a disservice to ourselves.

Our Spiritual Instincts are derived from within, giving us the ability to tap into positive or negative Spirituality and the Kingdom of Heaven. Yet, we as individuals must know and understand the difference. If not, we will confuse righteousness with unrighteousness, and vice versa, while appearing right in our own eyes.

In the Kingdom, right is right, and wrong is wrong without having a sliding scale. So, if we want the *Win-Win* to avail itself, it is crucial to stay on the righteous side of the spectrum, ensuring we are not oppressing others to appear as a winner. Plus, if we somehow step out of bounds, we want our Spiritual Instinct to kick in, alerting us to exercise extreme caution.

Can our Spiritual Instincts really become an alarm clock for the human psyche? Absolutely. However, it works both positively and negatively; therefore, it is best to become ONE with the Holy Trinity to ensure we are properly aligned with the Heavenly of Heavens. If not, we can become misled by something or someone appearing godly but sent straight from the Pit to wreak havoc. At the same time, turning what we know as Spirituality into a joke, especially if we are not synced into the Fruits of the Spirit and Christlike Character. How is this possible? First, if we do not know we have power over any foul spirit, we are already defeated in their eyes until we come to ourselves. Secondly, to create a *Win-Win*, we must know there is one. Thirdly, if we do not know the fight is fixed, we will throw up a flag, surrendering to it.

Listen, once again, the *Win-Win* is already in our DNA; we need to find it and use it. How? The Holy Trinity (The Father, Son, and Holy Spirit) is here to help us; all we need to do is accept the help, listen, learn, document, and sow back into the Kingdom when the time is right. We do not need to get all complicated and technical about the *Win-Win* because what we need is already.

- ☐ The *Healing* we need is already.
- ☐ The *Love* we need is already.
- ☐ The *Breakthrough* we need is already.
- ☐ The *Blessing* or *Birthright* we need is already.
- ☐ The *Provision* we need is already.
- ☐ The *Information* we need is already.
- ☐ The *Know-How* we need is already.
- ☐ The *How-To* we need is already.
- ☐ The *Spiritual Fruits* we need are already.
- ☐ The *Wisdom* we need is already.
- ☐ The *Helpful Intervention* we need is already.
- ☐ The *Motivational Illumination* we need is already.

All in all, we must master our ability to take possession of what or who rightly belongs to us. Before we move on, just because it is ALREADY does not mean we are adequately prepared to receive. For this reason, we need the Holy Spirit as a formal Spiritual Guide, helping us filter out the negative worldliness. Meanwhile, ushering in Kingdom Positivity with the Divine Covering of the Blood of Jesus.

How do we extract what is ALREADY? The best way to extract and convert is to begin to ask ourselves fact-finding questions in the *What, When, Where, How, Why*, and with *Whom* Formation, talking it out with ourselves while documenting what comes out. If we do this for 40 days without fail, we will find that what we thought was the issue affecting our *Win-Win* is really not it. By questioning the human psyche to yield the vital information or truths needed to extract and convert negatives into positives, the *Win-Wins* get easier as time progresses.

We can get all Spiritual with the extracting and converting process. But the truth is, we use Spirituality as a smokescreen to cover up or downplay our senses, predicated on the lust of the eyes, the lust of the flesh, and the pride of life. How do we use this in such a manner? We tend to point the finger at others to take the heat off ourselves, not realizing we all have issues in need of reckoning. As a result, we develop a Mindset of Perfection instead of a Workable, Transformative, and Positive Mindset.

When in all actuality, according to the Heavenly of Heavens, it is imperative to remove all smokescreens associated with any form of masks or coverups. Transparency is the key to creating a *Win-Win* on any level. Really? Yes, really. When we are full of lies, the conscience remembers, and it secretly holds it against us, especially when we want to do the right thing or put the human psyche on lockdown for Spiritual Edification or Renewal.

So, based upon the lies we are telling ourselves or the hidden issues we whitewash, the psyche retaliates, rejecting the *Win-Win* with superfluous doubt. What does this mean? Typically, this is when the silent inner chatter becomes deafening, clouding our sense of reasoning and good judgment, pulling us from pillar to post, not knowing if we are coming or going. Whereas, if we are transparent, when the psyche begins to torment us or become a little tattletale, we must boldly do a few things, but not limited to such:

- ☐ Give thanks for the learning process while acknowledging our Heavenly Father.
- ☐ Invoke the presence of the Holy Spirit to permeate the Mind, Body, and Soul with His presence.
- ☐ Repent of any provocations or Triggers associated while reversing the negative into a positive.
- ☐ Cover the DOORPOST of every thought, feeling, emotion, sense, or desire with the Blood of Jesus.
- ☐ Say 'I am a work-in-progress, creating a *Win-Win* out of ___'
- ☐ Quote the Biblical Scripture associated.

- ☐ Use positive affirmations.
- ☐ Place a Spiritual Seal by saying, 'Amen.'

Without a doubt, we have what we need; still, we must master the ability to interject the Spiritual Principles required to cause the *Win-Win* to yield on our behalf or work in our favor.

It is often said, 'Favor is not fair.' However, when dealing with a *Win-Win*, 'Favor is Just.' What does this mean? We have the power to create favorable conditions by involving the Holy Trinity, applying the Word of God, using the Fruits of the Spirit, and exhibiting Christlike Character.

Listen, if the worldly system can create or groom a person to behave sensibly when in public settings through proper etiquette. We, too, can do likewise from a Kingdom Perspective to have lasting effects in or out of the public and Kingdom arenas through the use of Spiritual Etiquette.

What can Spiritual Etiquette do for us? It gives us the confidence and astuteness needed to approach anyone with the Standards and Principles of the Kingdom without becoming repulsive, condescending, or offensive. Plus, it helps us exhibit the Fruits of the Spirit and Christlike Character in our people skills or communicative efforts.

Unbeknown to most, many Believers shy away from Spirituality due to the abrasive or condescending approach we have developed over the years. Yet, instead of them saying, 'Your behavior sucks.' They opt to leave the environment, traumatizing their psyche and putting themselves in a more compromising and confusing situation with God and their salvation.

And sadly, there are times when a devout Believer opts to go to the dark side for Mental, Physical, or Emotional comfort. The dark side knows the value of having great people skills. Therefore, they take the time to work on making their communicable efforts impeccable, recruiting what the Church threw away or rejected. Is this really happening? Of course. It is happening all too often.

Personally, I was one of those the Church rejected, not one time, but repeatedly. To be clear, I was not being rejected because I was a bad person, villain, hurting someone, misbehaving, an evil individual, or anything associated with any form of debauchery whatsoever. However, the rejection was GOOD for me. Why was it so good? Remember, I have mastered how to create *Win-Win Situations* since I was five years old, and I was not going to allow anyone or anything to block my Creative Abilities or Divine Ingenuity.

From my perspective, it meant I had a little more work to do in changing the trajectory of what was taking place. What type of work needed to take place? I took my Gifts, Calling, Talents, and Creativity to the Church, and they were rejected. And now, as the Heavenly of Heavens has shown favor to me, the Church or anyone associated with Spiritual Means must want what I have to offer to receive it. Is this a little arrogant? Absolutely not!

I give what the Heavenly of Heavens gave me freely, with no strings attached. Plus, irrespective of the *Win-Win*, I know the feeling of the impending trauma we face. What is more, I have much compassion for those who do not meet the standards of a certain Christian Environment, especially when we refuse to engage in evil acts of pouncing upon the innocent, or when we frown upon ungodly behavior.

For me, I was determined NOT to allow anyone or anything to come in between my Walk with God. So, to stay in Purpose on purpose with all of my Spiritual Gifts, Calling, Talents, and Creativity in hand, I had to develop a *Spirit to Spirit* Relationship with the Heavenly of Heavens. As my '*Give Back*' to the Kingdom, I have come back to Unveil the Veiled, bearing no grudges, showing others how to do likewise with the Holy Trinity at the forefront.

Listen, the best way to convert negatives into positives, wrong into rights, injustices into justice, bad into good, and so on, with all due respect, is to apply Spiritual Principles, not Churchy Principles. What does this mean? We must begin to align all things with the Divine Word, Will, and Ways of God, *As It Pleases Him*. If our fruits or behaviors are not adding up to the Kingdom Standards set in place according to the Word of God, it is best to regraft them with the Fruits of the Spirit. If not, it will hinder our Spiritual Walk.

According to the Heavenly of Heavens, regardless of what we are going through or have been through, it is not too late. We can start from where we are, repentantly taking one step or fruit at a time. Plus, it does not matter who rejects us amid our transformation; God will honor our wholehearted attempts to work on ourselves as we become a work-in-progress.

Besides, God will use anyone or anything to help and change the lives of others. Therefore, we should never count ourselves out, especially when we are indeed in the number. What does this mean? *"But the very hairs of your head are all numbered. Do not fear therefore; you are of more value than many sparrows."* Luke 12:7. If we avail ourselves to the Will of God while making a wholehearted attempt to use His Divine Principles. He will honor this, especially when we operate in the Spirit of Obedience and Humility. Really? Yes, really! Here is the Spiritual Decree, *"When you were few in number, indeed very few, and strangers in it. When they went from one nation to another, and from one kingdom to another people, He permitted no man to do them wrong; Yes, He rebuked kings for their sakes, saying, 'Do not touch My anointed ones, And do My prophets no harm.' "* 1 Chronicles 16:19-22.

In our *Spirit to Spirit* Relationship, we have more access to our Heavenly Father than we think. We simply need to get into His Presence alone with pen and paper in hand to document from the Heavenly Realm to our Earthen Vessels, allowing the Divine Wisdom to flow.

Will God in Three Persons really have a *Spirit to Spirit* Relationship with us? Absolutely, the same way I am documenting my notes for the edification of others to read in this book, anyone on the face of this earth can do likewise. Here is one of the Spiritual Decrees for *Spirit to Spirit* Relations, *"At that day you will know that I am in My Father, and you in Me, and I in you. He who has My commandments and keeps them, it is he who loves Me. And he who loves Me will be loved by My Father, and I will love him and manifest Myself to him."* John 14:20-21.

Now, before I end this chapter, for the commissioning of New Beginnings, here is the Spiritual Decree as well: *"Thus says God the LORD, Who created the heavens and stretched them out, Who spread forth the earth and that which comes from it, Who gives breath to the people on it, And spirit to those who walk on it: 'I, the LORD, have called You in righteousness, And will hold Your hand; I will keep You and give You as a covenant to the people, As a light to the Gentiles, To open blind eyes, to bring out prisoners from the prison, Those who sit in darkness from the prison house. I am the LORD, that is My name; And My glory I will not give to another, Nor My praise to carved images. Behold, the former things have come to pass, and new things I declare; Before they spring forth I tell you of them.'"* Isaiah 42:5-9.

Chapter Seven

NEW BEGINNINGS

How many times have we been dragged through the dirt for making an honest mistake? How often have we been put on blast for our good intent? Better yet, how often have we made wholehearted attempts to do the right thing for someone, and they turn around and spit in our face without saying, 'Thank You.' We all have had our share of something pushing us to the edge or dragging us away from our Passion. But all is not lost. Anything or anyone who has contributed to our shame, abuse, setbacks, lessons, or whatever has played its role. And, NOW it is time to revamp the *Win-Win* hidden in our *New Beginning*.

As we are out with the old and in with the new, we must know and understand that everything will work together for our good. Now, with a commitment to *New Beginnings*, speaking to ourselves in this manner, the psyche will begin to proactively admit or tell us the issues in need of work, revamping, or regrafting. Really? Yes, really! It is commonly called Spiritual Discernment. We all have this, but we often do not realize how it works on our behalf.

Once at the point of Discernment, when we add the Spirituality of the Holy Trinity into the equation, the enemy cannot contend with us. We are open to our issues while working on them to become better. At the same time, allowing grace, mercy, forgiveness, repentance, and the Blood of Jesus to work on our behalf as we become learners, doers, and sowers for the Kingdom through practical everyday living in our Earthen Vessels.

How do we *Begin Again*? Listed below are a few items to get rid of, but not limited to such:

- ☐ Get rid of envy, jealousy, and coveting.
- ☐ Get rid of pompousness.
- ☐ Get rid of anger.
- ☐ Get rid of greed.
- ☐ Get rid of selfishness.
- ☐ Get rid of disobedience.
- ☐ Get rid of competitiveness.
- ☐ Get rid of insecurities.
- ☐ Get rid of negativity.
- ☐ Get rid of rejection.
- ☐ Get rid of false expectations.
- ☐ Get rid of untruths.

Getting rid of these negative characteristics helps us become more confident in 'Who' we are and 'Why' we are. Once this happens, we will NOT have to depend on others for reassurance or validation. Instead, we can be who we are with no regrets; plus, we will not have the desire to be someone else or outright play pretend.

Amid our *New Beginnings*, we must involve the Holy Trinity in the equation to align us with our Divine Blueprint. In the grand tapestry of life, it saves time and energy, keeping us from redoing things we can get right the first time around. In addition, it also prevents us from getting out of character, especially when we are called to a higher standard.

To ensure Divine Understanding, after the initial *New Beginning*, if we need to *Begin Again*, do it! Just make sure repenting is taking place. Why do we need to *Begin Again*, over and over? Some are able to get it right the first time around, and some have to start over several times until they get it right. Personally, I happened to be one of those individuals who had to *Begin Again* several times until I got it right; therefore, the forgiveness, mercy, and compassion I have for others made the journey well worth starting over and over until I mastered the *Art of Newness*.

Here is the deal: The *Art of Newness* is predicated on proactively waking up every day to a fresh start. So, instead of waiting to fall short, I change my Mindset to start every day with a clean slate, repenting and getting rid of yesterday's sludge with a new Kingdom Mindset. By doing so, it keeps me from saying, 'I blew it again.' Listen, there is a *Win-Win* hidden in every day, and if we cannot find it, do not worry; a fresh mindset brings New Revelation.

Does the *Art of Newness* really work? Absolutely. Basically, this is how I write under the Anointing of the Holy Spirit. What does this mean? What I write about today does not necessarily bring the full Spiritual Revelation on the same day. For this reason, I have to RESET myself to receive my Daily Bread or Portion hidden in that day, creating a *Win-Win* with what is present. If I do not receive anything, I do not force it.

Yet, when the Floodgate is open, I am disciplined enough to capture it, while knowing the *New Beginnings* of Divine Wisdom for the next day will avail itself. Besides, according to the Heavenly of Heavens, as long as I am at peace with myself and others, the Well of Wisdom will flow without fail to create a *Win-Win* in my life and the lives of others.

Listen, when operating in the Realm of the Spirit, if we become humbly obedient, repenting, and respectful, the Well of Wisdom will open on our behalf as well, especially when we understand every day is designed to take care of itself. If we have a hard time believing this, just take a look at the Cycle of Nature. Even through much neglect on our behalf, Nature takes care of itself based on the Divine System set in place from the Beginning.

In my opinion, if we respect the power associated with the Beginning, we are better able to respect and understand the ending of whatever or with whomever. Listen, the Cycle or Vicissitudes of Life do not stop because we have a temper tantrum; it continues with or without our permission. And, if we decide to wallow amid the changes, then that is our free will choice. But we cannot lay the blame elsewhere when we become stuck in the same season for years or settle for a lose-lose, especially when the *Win-Win* is available.

When engaging in a *New Beginning*, it is best to focus on a step-by-step journey through Mind Mapping. By doing so, it helps us to understand our new journey without taking giant leaps we do not understand. If we do, it may leave us scratching our heads in dismay when it does not work out according to what we envisioned. Whereas, if our goals are documented through Mind Mapping, we can quickly pinpoint our point of misdirection, confusion, fear, inadequacy, dissatisfaction, or distraction.

In addition, when Mind Mapping, we can better understand our Divine Blueprint while self-evaluating accordingly. With this process, it also helps to enhance our instinctual decision-making abilities associated with becoming Spirit-Led. It builds trust and structure within the human psyche, helping us relax amid chaos and confusion, knowing the *Win-Win* is already in our favor.

As I stated earlier, when dealing with the Holy Trinity, we may not get all the details at once; therefore, we must find a system to keep track of the information given. Once we become a good steward over what we are given, the Heavenly of Heavens will usher in more information for us to process in stages, building our Level of Spirituality.

Why do we need Spirituality? We are Spiritual Beings having a human experience, so we must RESPECT this fact. If not, we become limited to certain details of our DNA, Divine Blueprint, or Spiritual Benefits.

Our Plan of Action or Plan of Strategy will always work best when we incorporate Spiritual Means to edify or plant Seeds of Goodness. What if we are not Holy Ghost-Filled and Fire-Baptized? God will use anything or anyone to Bless His Kingdom or His sheep; therefore, it is not my responsibility to pass judgment on what or who He may use. My goal is to convey the right things to do, do my part as it relates to my Divine Blueprint, and do all things in the Spirit of Righteousness and Excellence, leading everyone back to the Kingdom.

Becoming Spirit-Led is not something we would want to take for granted. To state it plainly, we, as Believers, are held to a higher standard than those who are reckless, carefree, naive, and misunderstood. We are called to lead the way in the Spirit of Righteousness, illuminating the path toward the Light. Conversely, if we are getting down and dirty in the Name of God, Kingdom Reckoning will soon call us out with a Spiritual Bull's-eye.

What is the purpose of being called out? Spiritual Recklessness or Misrepresentation is a big no-no in the Kingdom of God. From my perspective, it is a Spiritual Booby-Trap waiting for the right time to put us in a timeout. For this reason, it is best to start over in a fully repented state of being with the Holy Trinity at the forefront, using the Fruits of the Spirit and exhibiting Christlike Character. By doing so, it allows us to grow and mature according to the Standards of the Kingdom without filling in the gaps by doing our own or the wrong thing, pleasing ourselves.

Listen, when operating in the Spirit of Excellence or searching for the *Win-Win*, we do not want to become clouded or confused with any form of folly, especially when we are Spirit Led. The Holy Spirit will lie dormant with self-induced folly, foolery, waywardness, confusion, disobedience, or debauchery. So, if we want to enter the Kingdom of Heaven in a bed of unrepentant negativity, we are in for a rude awakening. The Vicissitudes of Life will pressure us to step into the Spiritual Classroom or take a step back until we are ready to begin again in the Will of God, not the will of man.

If we think for a minute, we can run the Kingdom of Heaven like we run our earthly affairs, we are sadly mistaken. Once again, we are NOT required to be perfect, but willful accountability, transparency, and repentance are a must. If we are not willing to change for the better, the Spiritual Transformation cannot fully occur.

Regardless of our opinion of God, He is not going to violate our will; we must want a *New Beginning* for ourselves. What if we are a little rough around the edges, and we are in need of a little help with Spiritual Etiquette? No one is perfect; however, if we use the Fruits of the Spirit to build our Christlike Character, it will put us on the Leading Edge. Just take one Spiritual Fruit at a time; once perfected, then move to the next. It worked for me, and I promise it will work for anyone who makes a wholehearted attempt to become a work-in-progress with the Holy Trinity at the forefront.

Let us take *New Beginnings* a step further. As we maneuver through our journey, we must love everyone we encounter, putting all forms of judgment to the side. To be clear, this is not the lustful type of love; it is the brotherly or sisterly type of love, caring, and compassion. Even if people pretend they do not recognize a loving heart, they do! Love bridges the gap in our Saving Grace.

Once we perfect the Art of Love, we must put away the negative or critical innuendos, especially when disappointed. Regardless of where we are in life or what we have done, the human psyche secretly responds to encouragement. Unbeknown to most, amid disciplining, if someone understands the true reasoning in the *What, When, Where, How, Why,* and with *Whom* Formation, with a little underlying conversational encouragement to do better, they will respond, even if they pretend not to. Although it may take a little longer with this approach, the understanding is well worth the time spent, guaranteed. Not only will we help them understand our level of disappointment, but we will also help ourselves in the process.

As we take this a step further, regardless of our level of disappointment, we must refuse to complain, act like a fool, get out of character, or show our true colors. Self-control is extremely important, and if we feel ourselves about to boil over, we must put ourselves in a timeout until we calm down. Once we are rational, if we need to make a statement, say it positively with a proposed solution, understanding, or advice. In other words, if we cannot contribute to the situation positively, we should take a step back until we can.

How do we know if we are calm? It is often unveiled when we can become grateful for the experience and think positively and rationally. If the inner chatter is still raging out of control or experiencing a flood of negative thoughts, we are not ready. We have to set a higher guard over the negative thoughts or emotions by some form of Spiritual Counteraction. We can use the Word of God, positive affirmations, convert negatives into positives, and repent of the negative thoughts or emotions gone wild.

Now, once we are ready to approach or respond to the situation, if it needs one, then we should extend gratefulness, respect, and humility. If we cannot show or extend any of the three, it is imperative to deal with the hidden SEEDS of ungratefulness.

Why do we have to jump through hoops to become the bigger person? According to Kingdom Standards, we must make everyone feel as if they are important, even if they are not. Why would we mislead someone in this manner? Which is better, to treat them as if they are worthless or to treat them with dignity, honor, and respect? What truly matters in the Eye of God is which behavior do we think He would BLESS, or which one would have a profound positive effect or outcome? After all, people will always remember how we made them feel; even if they forgive us, they still have the capacity to remember. Notably, if we desire to have the Heavenly of Heavens to smile upon us, KINDNESS is the way.

For the record, before we get out of character, we must remember that we symbolically treat others how we secretly treat ourselves when no one is looking. Here is what we need to know: *"A good man out of the good treasure of his heart brings forth good; and an evil man out of the evil treasure of his heart brings forth evil. For out of the abundance of the heart his mouth speaks."* Luke 6:45.

The authentic approach to importance begins within us and then spreads outwardly. In the grand tapestry of life, if we want to be treated as if we are important, we must share the charactorial traits of it, making others feel important, even if we do not feel as if they are worth the effort. Besides, sharing it is not for them; it is for us. Here is the scripture we need: *"Give, and it will be given to you: good measure, pressed down, shaken together, and running over will be put into your bosom. For with the same measure that you use, it will be measured back to you."* Luke 6:38.

What if we choose not to do the right thing? Can we just ask for forgiveness? Of course, we can ask for it. Know this: Regardless of how we feel, we should want to always operate in the Spirit of Righteousness. Rest assured, there may come a time when the shoe is on the other foot, where we are seeking forgiveness as well. According to the Heavenly of Heavens, it is best to forgive and move on, knowing that in our moment of need, we will not be forgotten. *"Therefore, be merciful, just as your Father also is merciful. Judge not, and you shall not be judged. Condemn not, and you shall not be condemned. Forgive, and you will be forgiven."* Luke 6:36-37.

Chapter Eight

ACTIONABLE BEHAVIORS

Everything we do, say, or become is surrounded by some form of action, reaction, thought, or belief. If we do not recognize which one of the behaviors we exhibit, we leave an open door for the enemy to create an illusion of a lose-lose situation instead of a *Win-Win*. As It Pleases God, we must become conscious about what we are doing or how we behave on a personal level before it makes its way into reality.

Once our behaviors become normal, it is harder to break the negative ones or reverse the damage. If we do not see a problem with behaving negatively, we will not recognize it as such, or we will support those behaving in this manner as well. So, it is best to proactively self-correct with the Fruits of the Spirit and Christlike Character, ensuring we are putting forth our best selves and building others along the way.

The *Win-Win* does not expect everyone to be perfect in analyzing every thought, action, behavior, or reaction. Yet, when aligning ourselves with a Kingdom Mindset, we are expected to use the Fruits of the Spirit to fill in the gap between what we know and understand and what we do not. From my perspective, exhibiting the Fruits of the Spirit and Christlike Character is like having gap insurance, covering us when we fall short. For this reason, it is always best to put in the work on the front end, ensuring we have fewer liabilities on the back end.

Beyond a shadow of a doubt, the self-examination of any *Win-Win* goes far beyond recalling what happened to us. It is about reeling in and understanding what is happening within us. Now, to effectively do so, the mind must become more geared toward *Spiritual Principles*. Worldliness is not going to get it, especially when the world did not create itself. We must look closely at the reflection of our thoughts, actions, reactions, feelings, attitudes, beliefs, motives, experiences, and objectives from the Eye of the Kingdom.

By doing so, we will begin to understand and master the Fruits of the Spirit, as they will give us clues on how to act, react, and conduct ourselves in any situation with Christlike Character, while resulting in fewer negative Triggers. Why would we have less harmful Triggers? We can see the *Win-Win* when others see defeat. Plus, we will have faith in knowing that all things will work together for our good for real.

With our *Actionable Behaviors*, we must ensure we are not the only ones incorporated in the *Win-Win*. If our *Win-Win* is all about us, it means self-centeredness is in the camp. However, if we desire to create profitable *Win-Win Situations*, we must refocus our mindset to Kingdom-Centeredness. How do we go about doing so? Listed below are a few must-knows, but not limited to such:

- ☐ We must know if we are taking action and what actions we are presumably taking.
- ☐ We must know if we are reacting and why we are doing so.
- ☐ We must know what we are thinking, why we are thinking in such a manner, and whether we should keep the thought, process it, reverse it, or discard it.

- ☐ We must know if we are being transparent with ourselves and others, or if we are wallowing in a whole bunch of untruths.
- ☐ We must know what we believe, why we believe, and how it affects us or others.
- ☐ We must know and understand how we are feeling and what makes us feel this way.
- ☐ We must know if we are operating in fear or doubt and what is causing it.
- ☐ We must know what fruits are associated with our *Actions* or *Behaviors*.

What is the purpose of knowing the above items? It prevents certain types of *Actionable Behaviors*. Plus, we do not want people to cringe when we show up or open our mouths to speak. Instead, the goal is to have an edifying presence about us, causing people to want to see us or hear what we have to say.

In the Kingdom, our character is of the utmost importance. Realistically, it helps us to deal with self-defiant behaviors that have the potential to contaminate our Win-Win or the Mind Mapped Goals associated with bringing them into reality.

We must understand that unmet goals or failure cause a cloud of secret or open depression, dissatisfaction, or feelings of unworthiness for the untrained or negative mind. We want to squash this mentality for *The Win-Win of Divine Greatness*, taking our Positive Mindset to the next level. Just keep in mind, "*A disciple is not above his teacher, but everyone who is perfectly trained will be like his teacher.*" Luke 6:40.

What *Actionable Behaviors* are in question by the Heavenly of Heavens? Listed below are a few indicators, but once again, not limited to such:

- ☐ When we cannot keep our word, or we are wishy-washy.
- ☐ When we are rude, pushy, or manipulative.
- ☐ When we have an atrocious or disrespectful attitude.

- ☐ When we become desensitized to the feelings of others.
- ☐ When we disrespect the elements of time.
- ☐ When we complain about everything or are not being satisfied.
- ☐ When we gossip, destroying the lives of others.
- ☐ When we are ungrateful, taking people, places, and things for granted.
- ☐ When we are unforgiving, holding all types of grudges, or exhibiting hatefulness.
- ☐ When we use traumatization as a weapon of control.
- ☐ When we ignore others to self-promote.
- ☐ When we use and abuse others as if we do not have a conscience.

Unbeknown to most, from a Spiritual Perspective, our negative *Actionable Behaviors* make us feel unworthy, unsuccessful, and undeserving, leading to all forms of Spiritual Unlawfulness. As a result, we put a monkey wrench in our efforts to reverse anything into a *Win-Win*.

How is it possible to put a monkey wrench in our efforts, especially when we are indeed on the winning end? It is possible to seemingly win when we are playing dirty or misbehaving; however, we must also take our motives of the *Win-Win* into account. So, if we win on the front end or in front of people and lose on the back end, is it really a *Win-Win*? Point in fact, I am not here to judge the *Win-Win*; I am here to help establish the attainable and sustainable *Win-Win* from the inside out through having a Positive Mental Mindset, causing all things to work together for our good.

Meanwhile, if we develop our positive *Actionable Behaviors*, it helps us reverse negativity into positivity, giving us a choice to engage in Spiritual Righteousness. Doing so allows us an opportunity or unction to endure the journey of creating a *Win-Win*, especially when the perception of others is locked on defeat. More importantly, it also helps us become a work-in-progress, allowing us the opportunity to self-correct instead of self-destruct.

Our Positive Mental Mindset is a choice of accountability; actually, it is a workable choice available to all, only used by a few, and the uses are claimed by most. All this means is that there is a lot of pretending going on, causing the inferiority complex to run wild. Frankly, with all due respect, this happens when we think everyone else has the problem while not taking the time to work on ourselves from the inside out. To be clear, these are not my words; here is what we need to know: *"And why do you look at the speck in your brother's eye, but do not perceive the plank in your own eye? Or how can you say to your brother, 'Brother, let me remove the speck that is in your eye,' when you yourself do not see the plank that is in your own eye? Hypocrite! First remove the plank from your own eye, and then you will see clearly to remove the speck that is in your brother's eye."* Luke 6:41-42.

Listen, if we are a chatterbox or on a soapbox more than we are listening, it is imperative to reverse this adverse behavior. If we talk, talk, talk just to hear ourselves speak, it is very difficult to process our thoughts effectively, to have effective conversational relations, or to understand what is or is not being said. As a result, we are quick to jump to conclusions based on our inability to understand or ask the right fact-finding questions.

Once we develop impeccable listening skills, hearing the audible and inaudible, we are better able to proactively create or extract the *Win-Win* out of any situation. Plus, it also gives us the ability to think on our feet or think about what we will say before it is said. How? It is in our nature to be understood, and if we fail to take the time to listen to what is being conveyed, we can indeed miss the mark in our communicative relations.

When we have a speaker and a listener in a conversation, there must be balance and understanding instead of a back-and-forth debate. If we dare to take our level of responding to the act of RELATING, it will cause people to open up to us instead of shutting down when we open our mouths. What does relating do for us? It helps us meet people where they are while keeping the conversation balanced, where we are not exhibiting immaturity and not being authoritatively bossy.

If we provide a conversationally safe zone, we can interject the Word or Love of God without them realizing it. How? When we effectively listen, people will symbolically tell us how to approach them. Listening to what they are saying is essential, but we must also listen to their tone, inflection, body language, eye contact, rhythm, and so on. What is the purpose of paying attention? *"Can the blind lead the blind? Will they not both fall into the ditch?"* Luke 6:39.

In the Kingdom, we do not have to beat someone over the head with the Bible; all we need to do is allow it to flow through us in our behaviors, thoughts, actions, reactions, and demeanor. If we are abrasively unkind and hateful when we approach people, they will respond or back up. It makes them uncomfortable. Some people will:

- ☐ React, lashing out to keep themselves safe.
- ☐ Backup, rejecting what we have to offer.
- ☐ Remain to contend or teach us a lesson.

In our *Actionable Behaviors*, we never want to put ourselves in a position to exhibit negative charactorial traits or talk down to ourselves or others. Degrading others on any level is a big no-no; we must find a way to build, using positivity instead of negativity. And if we do not have anything good to say, it is okay to plead the 5th. There is nothing wrong with holding our tongue; however, the problem arises when we unleash an ungoverned one.

How do we govern ourselves accordingly? We must hone in on our fruits and character. They are recognizable in our thoughts, actions, behaviors, reactions, words, demeanor, and countenance. Listed below are a few behavioral examples, but by no means limited to such:

- ☐ When we seek attention by any means necessary.
- ☐ When we lack interest in the well-being of others, especially if there is no form of benefit associated.

- ☐ When we laugh or mock the downfall or stumble of another without offering a helping hand, especially if it is within our ability to do so.
- ☐ When we have a desire to prove our worthiness or prove who is in charge.
- ☐ When we cast down anything that has nothing to do with us or we are an outright dream killer.
- ☐ When we are eager to block others from positive progression, proving them wrong, or to test their limitations.
- ☐ When we secretly seek revenge, plotting moments of payback.
- ☐ When we intentionally reject others, or we are dead-set on making them an outcast.

We must know when to draw the line in the sand on what we are saying, doing, and becoming to ensure we are not setting ourselves up to contradict the Will of God or Kingdom Standards.

What is the purpose of drawing the line in the sand, especially when we have free will to do, say, and become whatever with whomever? Simply put, we have the freedom to do whatever with whomever, but when it comes down to our fruits, we must keep in mind that we choose them as well. Therefore, we cannot complain about the harvest. *"For a good tree does not bear bad fruit, nor does a bad tree bear good fruit. For every tree is known by its own fruit. For men do not gather figs from thorns, nor do they gather grapes from a bramble bush."* Luke 6:43-44.

According to the Heavenly of Heavens, to truly make it to the top with our Divine Blueprint in hand, we must first master our *Spirit to Spirit* Relations. Secondly, we must become an expert in using positive people skills consistently with everyone we come in contact with. Thirdly, we must obtain and sustain the ability to inspire them Mentally, Physically, Emotionally, and Spiritually, directing them to the Positive *Win-Win* in the Spirit of Excellence.

All of this seems easy, right? Of course, but there is indeed a catch! We must practice and perfect ourselves first in order to lead the way. If we can prove ourselves right in effectively using the Fruits of the Spirit and Christlike Character, we will not have a problem sharing this same potential with others, similar to what I am doing now. What makes this so important? We are all on a learning curve, but if we share our Inner Greatness or Potential with others, they are more likely to accept the free will invitation to follow suit.

According to the Heavenly of Heavens, we are impeccable learners, and we are more apt to open up to those who have our best interests at heart. While dealing with our *Actionable Behaviors*, if the *Win-Win* takes our good to better, our better to best, and our best to Greatest, it is a journey well taken. Besides, who would reject Divine Greatness only to settle for defeat? Plus, if you have made it this far in this book, I know this is not you! Settling for mediocrity is not on your radar, and the Repertoire of Greatness is yours for the taking.

The Win-Win of Divine Greatness is all in our approach and MINDSET. More importantly, there is no law against sharing the Good News of the Kingdom. Therefore, when in doubt about anything or anyone, just *"Sing to the LORD, all the earth; Proclaim the good news of His salvation from day to day."* 1 Chronicles 16:23. With the *Promises of God* or *As He Promised*, amid the waiting or receiving phases of my life, I approach all things in outright humility, allowing whoever needs what I have to offer to gravitate toward me naturally. I do not push, pull, convince, or force; I share what God gave or gives me freely. We must want it for ourselves!

Yet, among my shareable efforts of my personable *Win-Wins*, my Mindset or Method of Operation is set on positivity, productivity, righteousness, and fruitfulness. At the same time, redirecting all things back to the GOOD, keeping everything in the Light, and aligned with the Kingdom. Remember, regardless of where you are or what you are doing, the *Win-Win* is waiting for your attention. So, do not give up or give in; press through to the Mark of a Higher Calling in Christ Jesus. You got this! So, let us Mind Map it accordingly, proving that the Greatness within you is already!

Chapter Nine

WHAT IS MIND MAPPING?

If we desire to capitalize on existing in a constant State of Winning, we must be willing to learn, set goals, strategize, develop plans, journal, share, and relax. With this list, it appears straightforward, right? Then, why are so many of us missing the mark, knowing nothing about how to Mind Map or develop a Plan of Action?

From my perspective, it is not like we do not know what to do...we are just having a hard time with the implementation phase. How do I know? I was one of those people, and I am not ashamed to admit it! So, as my *Win-Win*, this is my 'Give-Back,' helping those unaware of this privy information.

When we are distracted and lack focus from the inside out, we will find ourselves spending most of our time paying attention to someone else's life while symbolically blocking out our reality without realizing it. Unbeknown to most, by not extracting the *Win-Wins* in life, we consume our lives by putting on a show or masking ourselves as if we are on the Winning Edge. When, in all actuality, we do not have to prove anything to anyone but ourselves and God. Therefore, if we take the time to Mind Map our journey, we can better align ourselves with our Divine Blueprint without faking it.

Truthfully, living our lives out of purpose is one thing, but trying to prove ourselves worthy to others, having nothing to do with our Divine Blueprint, is another. How so? It causes us to miss the mark in and out of the Kingdom!

When living our lives cluelessly, we will commonly find ourselves thriving on or off the opinions of others. At the same time, subjecting ourselves to becoming brainwashed by negativity, debauchery, and confusion, contradicting the Will of God and our Divine Blueprint.

With or without a Mind Map, once deception is within us, it will contradict the true charactorial essence of who we are from the core of our being, affecting the human psyche. And, from a Spiritual Perspective, it is always best to plan our exit out of any form of deceptive measures. How do we go about doing so? Strategically, especially when we have a desire to extract the *Win-Win*. Once again, the *Win-Win* is a MINDSET!

How can we successfully change our Mindset, capturing the *Win-Win* while capitalizing on the Blessings life has to offer? According to the Heavenly of Heavens, when mastering our *Win-Win*, it is not about who is the smartest, wisest, richest, and most successful. Frankly, in the obtaining phase, it is all about who is the most effective, consistent, proactive, and purposeful, using their Gifts, Talents, and Creativity according to their Divine Blueprint for their Heaven on Earth Experience.

Then, in the sustaining process, it is based upon who is mentoring, nurturing, maximizing the Fruits of the Spirit, and exhibiting Christlike Character. How is it possible to do all of this at once? Once again, Mind Mapping is the best way to do so, and it assists in tracking our progress as well.

What is Mind Mapping? Mind Mapping is a way to take the mind on a journey to some sort of accomplishment or a *Win-Win*. In addition, we can also associate Mind Mapping with building, dismantling, revamping, or regrafting our thoughts, ideas, concepts, precepts, and so on.

When we Mind Map, it enhances our ability to visualize strategically, instead of allowing the mind to wander aimlessly or ungoverned. If the mind is not governed correctly, it has a way of creating illusions, be it true or untrue, giving way to our perceptions, biases, conditioning, or limitations. By allowing this to happen, we unawaringly transfer or downplay our God-Given Rights, permitting the psyche to take over or run the show. However, with a Mind Map, we can rationally document while getting an understanding of the *What, When, Where, How, Why,* and with *Whom* Formational Questions.

Most often, we do not think questioning ourselves is important. With a Mental Mind Map, it is crucial to help us deal with more facts than fiction. Clearly, a little fiction is necessary to break the ice, create a little humor, or develop our momentum. Still, the underlying foundation must be built upon factual information. If our Mind Map is predicated on the Seeds of untruth, then our Harvest will eventually follow suit.

In pursuing the *Win-Win*, a Mind Map is ideal in helping us to envision the vision. What does this mean? It helps us to hone in on our imaginative efforts from the inside out. What is the difference? The vision is an outward manifestation, and the envision is an inside one. So, for the sake of the *Win-Win*, a Mind Map helps us bridge the gaps between the two, or it can also assist us in unblocking them.

Yet, amid all, we must understand the underlying desire for whatever or whomever. What does this mean for us? We must know the 'Why' behind our efforts. If we fail to understand this one fact, it limits our sincere efforts.

How can we limit ourselves when we are putting in the work? If we fail to connect to our passion, we cannot connect to ourselves. Nor can it feed us the necessary information to fuel our inner drive. For this reason, most people give up or run on empty. Then again, they may jump from one thing to the next or live their dreams through someone else. The bottom line is that if we fail to connect relationally, we will find ourselves doing the right things for all the wrong reasons, creating disconnects from the inside out.

On the other hand, if we properly connect ourselves using the Win-Win approach to Mind Mapping, there are no limits to what we can achieve. Really? Yes, really! Listen, a Mind Map is a Spiritual Tool of simplicity, giving us the ability to structure or restructure based on our present-day information. What does this mean? The instructions may change based on the level of our understanding, environment, conditioning, training, teachability, comprehension, resistance, and so on. All in all, we must PAY ATTENTION, period.

According to the Heavenly of Heavens, regardless of where we are or what we are going through, we cannot allow any form of frustration to detour us from our journey. For this reason, our Mind Map serves as a tangible source of information, getting us back on track when we suffer some form of detour. Then again, it may be a viable way to recall what we may have forgotten. For the most part, we will all have our moments, so if this happens, do not feel bad. We must dust ourselves off, jump back on the path, and keep moving toward Greatness in the Spirit of Excellence.

When using a Mind Map, if we redirect our focus to PURPOSE or our Divine Blueprint, we will have less time trying to please, coax, or cater to those who are not a part of the plan, who are wreaking havoc, or who are intentionally sowing discord. As a result, we have more time to provide a service, solve problems, or transform negatives into positives, creating a *Win-Win* for all we come in contact with.

When developing a Mind Map, we must find the one that caters to our unique Blueprint. Listed below are a few ways to create one that will work in our favor, but not limited to such:

- ☐ We must place the goal, idea, thought, purpose, or concept in the center of the page to develop FOCUS on the SEED.

- ☐ We can use images, colors, symbols, or whatever we desire to keep us CONNECTED or CENTERED on the primary goal.

- ☐ We must create BRANCHES connecting us to the SEED, asking the *What, When, Where, How, Why,* and with *Whom* Formational Questions.

- ☐ We can have as many boxes as we like, providing different answers to each question. For some, a page will do, but for others, they may need a wall, depending upon the desired vision, goal, purpose, or whatever.

- ☐ We must document the Take-Away or Ultimate Achievement desired.

- ☐ Once done, for six days a week, we must provide the Reflective Thoughts regarding the primary reason for the Mind Map.

- ☐ We must use positive affirmations over our Mind Map, squashing all negative interjections. Mind Mapping for the *Win-Win* is a Positive Zone only!

- ☐ We must be willing to revamp often; no Mind Map is set in stone; it is a constantly evolving process of COMMITMENT. Without growth, we are already symbolically defeated until we unblock ourselves.

If our Mind Map from the first day looks the same way a month later with the same information, this should be a RED FLAG of some form of stagnation or blockage.

A Mind Map can be used in any way we so desire. So, outside of our goals or purpose, we may use a Mind Map for a few other things, such as, but not limited to:

- ☐ Brainstorming.
- ☐ Projects or Presentations.
- ☐ Studying or Research.
- ☐ Relationships or Marriages.

- ☐ Self-development.
- ☐ Decision-making.
- ☐ Power moves.
- ☐ Family or Event planning.
- ☐ Problem Solving.
- ☐ Inner Growth.
- ☐ Note-taking for writing an article, book, script, and so on.
- ☐ Unveiling our hidden Gifts, Calling, Talents, Purpose, or Creativity.

Regardless of how we use our Mind Map, it will prevent whatever we are doing from becoming messy or disorganized, while we become crystal clear about 'What' we are doing and our reasons 'Why.' Most often, it is the power behind our 'Why' that makes the Win-Win GREAT, creating an overflow of Blessings.

So, if we need to pinpoint the areas in need of revamping, additional questioning, or pruning, do it. Do not waste precious time wandering when you have the same opportunity to subdue, conquer, and WIN with the Spiritual Tools you already have in your hand.

By leading our Mind Map in outright humility, servanthood, self-control, diligence, love, and wisdom, we will not only become effective, but we can also create *Win-Win Situations*. Yes, *Win-wins* to benefit the lives of others, creating Double and Triple-Portion Blessings. Putting in the work will not only benefit us, but also Bless others to become a Blessing as well, causing our act of diligence to keep giving to create an overflow with a Legacy of Impact.

Here is the deal: It is always best to understand our Divine Blueprint. It bears mentioning that it includes our prepackaged Gifts, Calling, Talents, and Creativity as the Spiritual Tools needed to facilitate our Divine Blueprint. If we do not have a clue, then it is our responsibility to become clued in on what is already within. So, it will take a little soul-searching on our behalf, but it is indeed well worth the effort. Personally, I am not writing this book for us to get half of a portion; the goal is to receive FULL PORTIONS, period!

We are dealing with our *Win-Wins* and Divine Birthrights; therefore, we want all that God has already Predestined for us to have from the Beginning. Now, with or without a Mind Map, we can use the questions below to get the ball rolling on pinpointing our Gifts, Calling, Talents, Purpose, or Creativity:

- ☐ We can make a list of WHAT we love doing.
- ☐ We can make a list of WHY we love doing it.
- ☐ We can make a list of WHEN we love doing it.
- ☐ We can make a list of HOW we love doing it.
- ☐ We can make a list of WHERE we love doing it.
- ☐ We can make a list of WHO we love doing it with.
- ☐ We can make a list of our 'TAKE AWAYS' for the Spiritual Unveiling.
- ☐ We can make a list of our 'GIVE BACK' for the Spiritual Unveiling.
- ☐ We can make a list of our POSITIVE FRUITS.
- ☐ We can make a list of our NEGATIVE FRUITS.
- ☐ We can make a list of the CONVERTED negatives to positives.
- ☐ We can make a list of the WIN-WIN without setting limits on the mind.

Our Gifts, Calling, Talents, Purpose, or Creativity will vary from person to person with different meanings and instructions; therefore, it is always best to put in the hands-on work ourselves first. It ensures that someone else's inner desires do not lead us. Plus, if they have not gone through the previous chapters, educating themselves from the Heavenly of Heavens on the *Win-Win*, contamination can occur. So, exercise extreme caution when incorporating those who have not gone through Spiritual Processing. Or those who lack the understanding of the importance of having and maintaining a Positive Mental Mindset.

When Mind Mapping with our Divine Blueprint, we must follow the Spiritual Rules, exhibit Christlike Character, and be willing to move into our Purpose, utilizing our Spiritual Gifts, Creativity, or Talents. Furthermore, we must also correctly discern between right and wrong, positive and negative, just and unjust, as well as good and evil. Without being able to discern people, places, and things properly, we can become an easy target of prey for the predators. So, we cannot be ignorant of the devices used to sift us Mentally, Physically, Emotionally, and Spiritually. What makes this so important? If we are all over the place in or out of our *Mind Mapping Sessions*, we can subconsciously compromise a few things, such as, but not limited to:

- ☐ Our Spiritual Connection or Receivers.
- ☐ Our Spiritual Queries.
- ☐ Our Spiritual Answers.
- ☐ Our Spiritual Astuteness.
- ☐ Our Spiritual Integrity.
- ☐ Our Spiritual Understanding.
- ☐ Our Spiritual Respectfulness.
- ☐ Our Spiritual Boundaries or Depth.
- ☐ Our Spiritual Protocol.
- ☐ Our Spiritual Compatibilities.
- ☐ Our Spiritual Fruits.
- ☐ Our Spiritual Journey.

Often enough, we take many things for granted, but when it comes down to our *Mind Mapping Sessions*, we should not play around. Why should we not lollygag in this matter? It is the Spiritual Tonic we need to satiate the inner thirst of the unnecessary, potentially debilitating issues of life. If we do not perfect this process to the point of having a direct connection to God in or out of our *Spirit to Spirit* Relations, we cannot fault anyone. We all have the same opportunity to receive all God has to offer; we merely need to get out of our own way.

As It Pleases God: Book Series

When doing our due diligence in Mind Mapping, to gain access to the Secrets of Wisdom or Divine Insight, it is imperative to step into its flow. Plus, to better understand Spiritual Truths from God's point of view, we must avail ourselves to the process as well. Listed below is a Mind Mapping Sample, giving us an idea of how to develop our own.

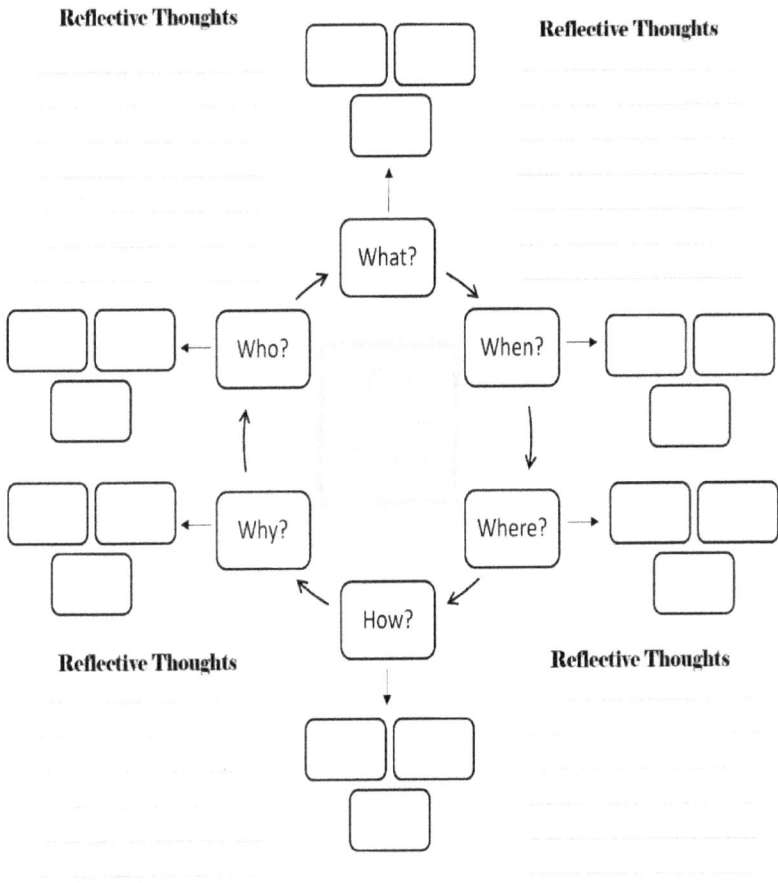

WHAT IS YOUR TAKE-AWAY OR ULTIMATE ACHIEVEMENT?

When Mind Mapping according to our Divine Blueprint, the Heavenly of Heavens wants us to double-check a few areas consistently:

- ☐ Double-check our thoughts.
- ☐ Double-check our emotions.
- ☐ Double-check our motives.
- ☐ Double-check our habits.
- ☐ Double-check our behaviors.
- ☐ Double-check our attitude.
- ☐ Double-check our decisions.
- ☐ Double-check our accountability.
- ☐ Double-check our idols.
- ☐ Double-check our lusts.
- ☐ Double-check our pride.
- ☐ Double-check our state of repentance and unforgiveness.

If we need to do a Mind Map for each one, do not be afraid to do it. It is our responsibility to take charge of our relationships with ourselves, ensuring we can request help in the areas of need or lack. Moreover, if we are already experts on ourselves, then congratulations! Nevertheless, those who desire to be their BEST self know what they have to do to achieve the *Win-Win* from within.

According to our Divine Blueprint, we must become a Spiritual Magnet in the *Win-Win*, allowing others to gravitate toward us freely. We cannot force our Divine Purpose on others, making them feel bad for not supporting us, or have our countenance fall when we do not receive what we expected.

More importantly, once we master the ability to listen and obey instructions, we will find our lives doing an about-face, giving our magnet a little more pulling force. What is the big deal about becoming a Spiritual Magnet? Simply because we are composed of magnetic properties with a natural positive or negative drawing force of our choosing.

If we desire to build our Magnetic Field in the Realm of the Spirit, it is best to begin to Mind Map our Spiritual Journey by praying and fasting on occasion, getting us from here to there...wherever our THERE is for us! Here is our *'here to there'* instructions: *"Then the disciples came to Jesus privately and said, 'Why could we not cast it out?' So Jesus said to them, 'Because of your unbelief; for assuredly, I say to you, if you have faith as a mustard seed, you will say to this mountain, 'Move from here to there,' and it will move; and nothing will be impossible for you. However, this kind does not go out except by prayer and fasting.'"* Matthew 17:19-21.

What do our Mountain, a mustard seed, fasting, and praying have to do with our Spiritual Magnet? According to The Win-Win of Divine Greatness, when Mind Mapping, our goal is to hit the targets, not miss them! If we have toxins blocking our Spiritual Magnet, it will not have the magnetic force needed to keep our faith alive to approach our Mountain or Valley when praying. Plus, if we are praying amissly, rest assured our fast is most often NOT targeted or Mind Mapped in the right direction. Wavering faith, emotions, thoughts, behaviors, and beliefs can get us caught up in desperation and doubt.

Furthermore, when we are desperate or doubtful, we become easy prey for our kryptonite to avail itself! So, beware. What would cause this to happen? Fear...the fear of the unknown has a way of debilitating those who are Spiritually Blind, Deaf, or Mute who do not realize they are.

The Win-Win of Divine Greatness will not allow us to play around as if we do not have a responsibility to become our highest and greatest self, doing all things in the Spirit of Excellence. Greatness holds us accountable for reaping the fruits of its labor. What does this mean for us? If Greatness is unveiled in our lives, then we must RESPECT it by giving, sharing, growing, and sowing back into the Kingdom with clean hands and a pure heart.

How do we ensure we are operating with clean hands and a pure heart? If we use the Fruits of the Spirit and Christlike Character at all times, self-correction will take place by default, bringing us into the Fold or Protection of God for further Spiritual Training or Mind Mapping as we make *Smart Moves*.

Chapter Ten

SMART MOVES

As the Cycle of Life requires change, so does the human psyche. Therefore, we must fine-tune the type of adjustments for the betterment of ourselves and others. According to the Ancient of Ancients, *Moving Smart* or *Smart Moves* have been around since the BEGINNING of time, under the guise of Wise Moves in the evolutionary or migratory process from the Garden of Eden, Noah's Ark, the changing of languages at the Tower of Babel, and so on. As we speed this up to today's time, we are now focused on internal moves, spreading outwardly to benefit the Kingdom of Heaven, *As It Pleases God*.

Can we find a way to uncomplicate things? Of course, we can. But the truth is, our complications are really a matter of perception, derived from within the human psyche, spreading outwardly. Once we begin to work positively on ourselves from within first, our outward experiences will change for the better by default. How? We will begin to see, hear, think, behave, and speak differently, geared toward the positive side of the spectrum. Whereas, if we continue to focus on negativity, we will change for the worse by default, becoming more complicated, confusing, and challenging to deal with. As a result, we become consumed by our senses, lusts, perversions, habits, competitiveness, and greed.

In this chapter, it is best to focus on the unseen to perfect what is visible to the naked eye. Why must we approach the complexities of life in such a manner? It helps us to narrow down the reasoning of 'What' affects us, 'Why' it affects us, 'How' it affects us, 'Where' it affects us, 'When' it affects us, and with 'Whom.' Whatever our 'it' is, there is always a SEEDFUL reason. If we do not narrow down the answers or query ourselves, it inadvertently becomes a seedless solution buried under layers of all types of debris.

To be clear, we all have something to work on or at; therefore, we should not point the finger at those working on themselves. Actually, in my opinion, it is well worth commending those who are intentionally working on themselves to become better people daily. Although better is a matter of opinion. Still, in the Eye of God, any progress in the right direction is a *Smart Move* instead of becoming complacent in a negative state of being. Here is the deal: The Kingdom of Heaven wants to know two things about us:

1. Whether we have *Pure Motives* of righteousness.
2. Whether we have *Tainted Motives* of unrighteousness.

We can complicate life as much as we want or play pretend all we like. But in the Kingdom, it boils down to two items leading up to our experiences in life, or the lack thereof. How is this possible when life is really complex? According to the Cycle of Life, everything has a SEED, whether it is a good or bad one.

For example, as a Seed to protect ourselves and our families, we now have the Smart Homes of today. And regardless of how we complicate the systems protecting our homes, we also have two questions as well:

- ☐ Whether our home is safe and secure, catering to our comfort levels.

As It Pleases God: Book Series

- [ ] Whether our home is unsafe and vulnerable, depriving us of a lifestyle of security.

These two SEEDFUL questions determine all other aspects of our conveyance system regardless of our projected outcomes.

On the other hand, when it comes down to the human psyche, we have become so complicated. According to the Heavenly of Heavens, we are dealing with right and wrong, just and unjust, good and evil, positive and negative, and so on. Yet, for some reason, we overlook our inner works, going straight to the outer works dealing with people, places, and things, catering to our senses, lusts, habits, biases, conditioning, and weaknesses. Plus, we are creating superficial issues having nothing to do with righteousness or unrighteousness, while jumping straight to justification or playing the blaming game without assuming total responsibility. Doing so contributes to a history of making bad or wrong moves instead of *Smart Ones*.

Neglecting to *Move Smart* contributes to our running from issues, situations, or people we need to deal with to bring healing or restoration from within. How is this possible, especially when we are living a great life? Living a great life is ideal, and if one has made it to this level, congratulations!

However, if we are dealing with any form of unforgiveness, anger, resentment, revenge, hatefulness, cruelty, jealousy, envy, pride, greed, or coveting, then we have work to do. Our psyche has not healed; it has buried issues that may hinder our walk with God, as we think we are right in our own eyes. What would cause this hindrance when we are devout Believers? It is the difference between living our truth and living a lie. Now, the question is, 'What are you living?'

Believe it or not, negative character traits hinder our walk with God, even if our works for God are perfect. What does this mean? Negativity affects the Fruits of the Spirit and our Christlike Character, regardless of our love for God. Blasphemy, right? Wrong. God takes note of how we treat people, especially the ones we think we do not need. Besides, most of our Spiritual

Testings will be with people or a situation, circumstance, or event surrounding them. From experience, I have seen more debauchery among Believers than unbelievers.

To take this a step further, as I operate in total humility throughout my journey, *Moving Smartly*, the Believers I encountered were unaware of my Level of Spirituality until after the fact. Or, better yet, for some, I would say, after the evil deed was done or after rejecting whatever I had to offer, then playing clean up once they found out. Respectfully speaking, more worldly individuals instinctively recognized my Spiritual Anointing than the Believers, doing anything to partake of it. The numbers baffled me back then, and they still do to this very day. To be clear, I love everyone, and I am very forgiving; however, according to the Heavenly of Heavens, we have to do better than this! In all humility, *Spirit knows Spirit*, and if one did not recognize the Spiritual Mark upon my life, it means they were not operating in the Spirit.

Unbeknown to most, when ranked in the Spirit at a certain level, respect must be extended naturally. If we cannot do so, it means we are Spiritually Blind, Deaf, or Mute. For this reason, we need to clear the channels of our *Spirit to Spirit* Connection to ensure we do not miss our Spiritual Cue, especially when we are making *Smart Moves*. For this reason, it is imperative to Spiritually See, Hear, and Speak the Language of the Kingdom while perfecting our Spiritual Instincts or Insight.

Now, regardless of our Level of Spirituality, God knows the heart of man; therefore, it is always best to repent of any and all negative character traits that have the potential to derail our walk with Him. By doing so, it allows the Holy Spirit to help us self-correct amid the moments we fall short. The human psyche tends to hide things from us. Meanwhile, the Holy Spirit exposes them, ensuring we can deal with whatever our 'it' is to enhance our developmental process.

When *Moving Smartly*, listed below are a few ways to *Move*, but not limited to such:

- ☐ *Move* with the Holy Trinity at the forefront.

- ☐ *Move* prayerfully and repentantly.
- ☐ *Move* respectfully and intuitively.
- ☐ *Move* humbly, peacefully, and consistently.
- ☐ *Move* in a state of forgiveness, mercifulness, and compassion.
- ☐ *Move* with an open, cautious, and caring demeanor.
- ☐ *Move* with the Fruits of the Spirit and Christlike Character in hand.
- ☐ *Move* in outright transparency, owning our truth.
- ☐ *Move* in confidence, knowing all things will work together for our good.
- ☐ *Move* in integrity and the Spirit of Righteousness, paying attention to what is happening around and within us.
- ☐ *Move* with a willingness to help others to do likewise, making our 'Give Back' epic.
- ☐ *Move* in total obedience while aligning ourselves with the Will of God or according to our Divine Blueprint, *As It Pleases Him.*

Unbeknown to most, true confidence comes from the Heavens Above! Once we make the Divine Connection, we are able to *Move Smart* in or out of the Will of God. Is it abominable to move outside the Will of God? Of course, especially without repentance or when we have committed to Him. But we all make mistakes, and for this reason, we have forgiveness, grace, and mercy. Plus, God will not violate our free will; we have to want 'it,' whatever our 'it' is for ourselves.

As the Vicissitudes of Life stake its claim, we will not be in the Will of God 100% of the time because we will all have our moments. Yet, amid all, we can become a 100% work-in-progress in and through Him. For those who attempt to convince me otherwise, red flags automatically go up of pending danger or a threat of a wolf in sheep's clothing. We cannot control what happens around us, and negative thoughts will come to distract or trick us, but it is our responsibility to Spiritually Counteract them or REPENT.

Truthfully, regardless of the picture of Holiness we are sold or have bought into, we cannot go from zero to one hundred in the Realm of the Spirit without being trained, tested, molded, and commissioned. People will get hurt due to our underlying and ungoverned worldliness appearing Spiritual, especially if we do not have a clue about our Spiritual Fruits or exhibiting Christlike Character. For this reason, in the Kingdom, we need the Holy Spirit to help us with Spiritual Principles; plus, we must have the Blood of Jesus as a Spiritual Covering, protecting us on the journey and while in the Spiritual Classroom.

More importantly, if we think we can do this on our own or contend with the wiles of the enemy without Spiritual Assistance, we are sadly mistaken. How? We are limited in what we can do without God. The moment we think we have arrived, most often, a Testing of the Spirit will appear. Therefore, if we place the Holy Trinity at the forefront of our lives, we can abound and rebound amid the Vicissitudes of life, keeping our heads held high.

Listen, we are the mere Earthen Vessel God uses to accomplish His Divine Purpose, but if we do not have any experience in building up and casting down, we become stuck in the Milking Stages. Plus, if we desire to get to the Spiritual Meat of the Kingdom, we must be able to effectively and succinctly use the Fruits of the Spirit and exhibit Christlike Character while in a state of full repentance. What is the purpose of being in a repentant state? We do not know what is around the corner to sucker punch us when we least expect it; thus, we must '*Stay on Ready*' at all times.

When moving in the Will of God, we need to put away negative character traits. The goal of *Moving Smart* is to stay Blessed with clean hands and a pure heart while NOT bringing shame to our household or name. For this, do not take my word for it; according to scripture, "*The curse of the LORD is on the house of the wicked, but He blesses the home of the just. Surely, He scorns the scornful, but gives grace to the humble. The wise shall inherit glory, but shame shall be the legacy of fools.*" Proverbs 3:33-35. With this knowledge from the Heavenly of

Heavens, we do not have to respond to everyone or everything. Just do the right thing and keep it moving in the Spirit of Excellence! The *Smart Move* path wants us to understand this: "*Do not be wise in your own eyes; fear the LORD and depart from evil.*" Proverbs 3:7.

In *Moving Smart*, we do not have to complicate our righteousness or settle for defeat, especially if we are Spiritually Awakened. All we need to do is focus on using the Fruits of the Spirit and exhibit Christlike Character, and the Holy Spirit will guide us the rest of the way.

Now, if we make a mistake or get something wrong, we should repent and plead the Blood of Jesus while getting to the ROOT of the matter. Then, we get back on track, governing our thoughts and emotions accordingly. Here is the *Moving Smart* Decree to keep close to us at all times, developing our *Mental Muscles*. "*Let not mercy and truth forsake you; bind them around your neck, write them on the tablet of your heart, and so find favor and high esteem in the sight of God and man. Trust in the LORD with all your heart, and lean not on your own understanding; in all your ways acknowledge Him, And He shall direct your paths.*" Proverbs 3:3-6.

Chapter Eleven

MENTAL MUSCLES

Our perceptional illusions are real beyond what we could possibly imagine, having the hidden Nuggets of Wisdom from the Heavenly of Heavens or Seeds of Destruction of our own making. Literally, the positive or negative images we play back to ourselves through our Mind's Eye can make or break us. It happens without us realizing it until the manifestation is right before our natural eyes.

If we dare to exercise our *Mental Muscles*, we will find that the Mind's Filtering Process will become very stringent and effective. The more we put in the work and exercise our Mental Capabilities, the more we can filter out the bad to make room for the good without making excuses.

According to the Heavenly of Heavens, we do not need to be a scholar to maximize our *Mental Muscles*. However, we do need to become willing and able to reach beyond our self-imposed limitations, putting our ego on the back burner to embrace humility, reachability, usability, and teachability. How can we go about doing so? We must hone in on our ability to transparently connect to people, places, and things to learn from them as they secretly or openly learn from us. By far, it will enhance our people skills by default, but it will also build Kingdom Trustworthiness as well. In addition, if the Heavenly of Heavens can genuinely trust us to shepherd, the Holy Spirit will train us in Kingdom Protocols, causing our *Mental Muscles* to grow in ways that will boggle the perception of those who are not privy to such information.

Now, before we move on, when dealing with our *Mental Muscles*, we must gain a grip on our perceptional illusions. The good or awkward feelings we have mean something, and we have to figure out or understand what that something is or is not. For example, a good feeling could be precisely what it is, or it could be a temporary filler of an inner or unresolved void. Then again, a bad feeling could be a forewarning from our instincts designed to protect us, or it could be an indication of insecurity, envy, jealousy, or coveting. For our sake, we must know the difference without any lingering doubts or second-guessing ourselves.

How is it possible to be on point with our perception? When building our *Mental Muscles*, we must be willing to have an honest *Q and A Session* with ourselves. It works wonders for the Mind, Body, Soul, and Spirit.

According to the Heavenly of Heavens, our *Mental Muscles* are also designed to help us deal with positive or negative triggers, traumas, lusts, thoughts, vices, wins, losses, detours, and so on. More importantly, it helps us deal with negative inner chatter or the hidden kryptonite we allow ourselves to endure in our moments of weakness.

The truth is, we all will go through the Vicissitudes of Life at some point where we lack understanding; we just need to equip ourselves to flex our *Spiritual Muscles* to stave off the wiles of the enemy. Why are we not using our *Mental Muscles* at this point instead of our *Spiritual Muscles*? First and foremost, we are all different. Secondly, our way of doing things may not work for everyone or the Kingdom. Thirdly, it may not align with our Divine Purpose, Blueprint, or the Will of God. Then again, we may need a character overhaul.

Furthermore, we need all the ammunition possible when life is throwing us a few curveballs. What type of ammunition do we need? We need the Spiritual Ammunition of the Holy Spirit. What can the Holy Spirit do for us, especially when life is shaking us to the core? The Holy Spirit can guide us in ways we could never guide ourselves, uprooting the hidden, non-conducive elements of the human psyche. Yet, when using our *Spiritual Muscles*, the Holy Spirit can help us pinpoint the additional *Muscles* needed to abase and abound or outright overcome. By approaching our issues in this manner, if we need to use our *Mental Muscles*, *Physical Muscles*, *Emotional Muscles*, or *Spiritual Muscles* simultaneously, consider it done!

Unbeknown to most, we all have the same rights to exercise our *Mental Muscles*, maximizing our *'Better to Best,' 'Best to Greatest,'* or Heaven on Earth Experience. Regardless of where we are in life or what we are doing, we cannot go wrong operating with a Positive Mental Mindset as long as we do not become demanding or controlling. Nor should we develop an addictive or clingy personality. Violating the free will of another really changes the rules of the game! If God does not violate our will, He does not expect us to behave in such a manner.

Teaching, guiding, mentoring, disciplining, or molding our children is totally different from violating the free will of another, especially when bending their will to satiate our selfish needs, wants, desires, or lusts. What is the big deal? First, we do not all have the same needs, wants, and desires. Secondly, we do not think alike or have the same taste. Thirdly, we bring harm or trauma to those who feel violated. And lastly, if we cannot deal with the free-willed freedom of another or their choices, then it is best to keep it moving.

Listen, we are not God, nor should we play God in the lives of others, altering their Divine Destiny to suit what we envision, as if they do not have a say-so in whatever or with whomever. What if we are trying to help them? We must incorporate them into the equation; if not, the web we are weaving can cause us to become caught up, feeling used, unappreciated, unloved, or rejected.

How can we avoid violating someone's free will? First, we must understand that we are relational beings; therefore, we must break the ice with effective communication. Secondly, we must listen to their wants, needs, desires, concerns, and so on. Thirdly, we must pride ourselves in asking the right fact-finding questions while gathering more information or developing an understanding, *As It Pleases God*. Then, finally, we must seek their permission with a formal or common ground agreement. Doing so helps us avoid engaging in a free will violation.

What if we are trying to surprise someone? Once again, we must listen and learn their likes and dislikes, needs and wants, and so on. But most of all, we should ask fact-finding questions, gaining a symbolic agreement without revealing the surprise. Does it work? Absolutely, it works better than buying something someone does not want or cannot use. In my opinion, this is why we get a lot of recycled gifts as opposed to having them prized or treasured. Here is the deal: When exercising our *Mental Muscles* regarding free will gifting, we need to know:

- ☐ People do not usually get rid of people, places, and things they have developed a valued connection to.
- ☐ People appreciate us paying attention to their wants, needs, and desires.
- ☐ People remember when we proactively take care of a need before having to ask.
- ☐ People secretly frown upon their '*Do Not*' wants.

According to the Heavenly of Heavens, violation of the free will of another has become the kryptonite of the century without us realizing it. How is this possible? Not gaining any form of agreement, intentionally manipulating, wishing ill will, or outright bullying opens the door to the dark side. What does this mean? It is a silent form of witchcraft. Really? Yes, really. So, be careful.

Whenever we bend or alter the will of another without their permission, it changes the Spiritual Rules, especially in the

Kingdom. Therefore, we must develop our *Mental Muscles* on how to approach situations, circumstances, and events with Spiritual Empowerment without master manipulating in the Name of God or some form of superficial guise. Most curses are coming from those who do not realize what they are doing while pleading the Blood of Jesus at the same time.

To add insult to injury, when engaging in debauchery, some actually think they are doing the right thing in their own eyes, claiming God told them this, and He told them that. While at the same time, not realizing that their fruits are revealing who said what! How do we know the difference? It is determined by good vs. bad, right vs. wrong, positive vs. negative, righteous vs. evil, love vs. hate, peace vs. chaos, and so on! Listed below are a few indicators to determine if we need to work on ourselves, but not limited to such:

- ☐ If our character is not Christlike, we have work to do.
- ☐ If our fruits are spoiled or negative, we have work to do.
- ☐ If we are having bouts with uncontrollable anger, we have work to do.
- ☐ If we are dealing with an out-of-control tongue, we have work to do.
- ☐ If we are unruly, we have work to do.
- ☐ If we are disrespectful or think we are above God, we have work to do.
- ☐ If we are addicted to drama or chaos, we have work to do.
- ☐ If we are control freaks, we have work to do.
- ☐ If we are egocentric or insensitive, we have work to do.
- ☐ If we are very judgmental or lack a conscience, we have work to do.
- ☐ If we are uncaring, hateful, or out of control, we have work to do.

Our *Spiritual Muscles* are designed to strengthen us, not make us weak, emotional, reactive, or intolerable. If, for some reason, we find ourselves contradicting our righteous beliefs, it is an indication that resentment, anger, or unforgiveness is residing in the heart. Whether we attempt to hide it or not, it becomes apparent in our actions, reactions, thoughts, demeanor, or communicable efforts. How do we reverse this? We must find the root of our issues and then Spiritually Regraft them. In my opinion, this is similar to skin or muscle grafting, which removes the old or damaged skin and then transplants and reprograms the new.

To be clear, when restructuring our *Mental Muscles*, choosing positive responses over negative ones cannot be forced upon us. We must want to do this for ourselves! We must use our own stimuli to create a positive *Gravitational Pull* from within the human psyche. If not, nothing changes because we will continue to attract negative energy. And, with enough pressure, we will explode or implode. What would cause this to happen? It is an outward expression of what we are feeling or experiencing from within. Once triggered without the barriers of self-control in place, we spew out the heart's contents or exhibit disruptive behaviors, telling everyone what is really going on from the inside out. How do we regraft our *Mental Muscles*? The regrafting process will vary from person to person. Yet, listed below are some of the basic 'Must Learns' to Spiritually Seal our growth process, but not limited to such:

- ☐ We must learn how to exhibit unconditional *Love* with no strings attached by freely giving and receiving love.

- ☐ We must learn how to obtain and maintain our level of *Peace*, and then share our peaceful energy outwardly.

- ☐ We must learn how to stir up the *Joy* from within the human psyche or spark the Creative Genius from within. By doing so, it helps to bring forth the inner excitement that only a few people allow themselves to experience.

- ☐ We must learn how to be *Patient* with ourselves and others. We are all a work-in-progress; therefore, we can learn, give, do, and share more of who we are from the inside out if we are patient. What makes this so important? Impatience disrupts and traumatizes the human psyche, having no respecter of persons. If we want to know why we are avoiding, this is a great place to start!

- [ ] We must learn how to exhibit *Kindness* in all things and with everyone. In today's time, we are being conditioned to think kindness is a weakness; however, according to the Heavenly of Heavens, it is by far a great strength hidden in plain sight. If we have never taken the time to be kind, we will never know or experience the Spiritual Benefits associated with this Heavenly Commodity.

- [ ] We must learn how to exhibit *Goodness*. It behooves us to become respectable people with good morals, great conduct, and impeccable character. When we are worthy of our Heavenly Merit, there is no limit on the Divine Favor bestowed upon our lives.

- [ ] We must learn how to exhibit *Faithfulness*. Our faith bridges the gap to all things Spiritual, even with our imperfections. Unbeknown to most, our Kingdom Value is built on being faithful. What can we expect from doing so? According to scripture, it says, *"Well done, good and faithful servant; you were faithful over a few things, I will make you ruler over many things. Enter into the joy of your Lord."* Matthew 25:21.

- [ ] We must learn how to become *Gentle* in our approach to all things. When we are gentle with our thoughts, words, demeanor, actions, reactions, and so on, we can extend it to others through the power of touch. Roughing people up or ruffling their feathers is a quick way to get pushed to the sideline in the Kingdom. Respect is a must! Without it, we already know what time it is.

As It Pleases God: Book Series

☐ We must learn how to exhibit *Self-Control* Mentally, Physically, Emotionally, and Spiritually. If we walk around as if we are a ticking time bomb or a loose cannon, we cannot expect people to hang around us unless they are just like us, they are using us, or they are benefiting from us in some way. Most often, it is through material gain, unresolved hunger and thirsts from within, or idolatry that causes a person to place themselves in harm's way intentionally or to knowingly become the next victim.

☐ We must learn how to kindly say 'No' to people, places, and things disrupting or detouring the human psyche. In addition, we must also learn how to pump the brakes on whatever is causing a disconnect in our Kingdom Relationship or Divine Blueprint.

☐ We must learn how to compassionately forgive, exhibiting mercy at the drop of a dime. Why should we forgive when we have been hurt, used, traumatized, and abused? If we desire to break the cycle, we must forgive, let go, and move on to become better. Holding on to unforgiveness, hatefulness, and revenge allows negative cycles to continue with our permission.

How do we permit a cycle that we did not create? By not learning, becoming better, or breaking the negative cycle, we symbolically join it. How is this possible when we are the victims? Unbeknown to most, it is done by secretly or openly suppressing the manifestation of negativity from within. It gives common ground for the energy to transfer to another, creating the same type of negativity, but in a situation, circumstance, or event that appears different to the natural eye. But it is still under the same label in our Spiritual Eye.

The bottom line is that in any form of negativity or whether it has left a bad taste in our mouths, we have the same opportunity to break it through forgiving, converting it into a positive, learning the lesson, and then growing to create a *Win-Win*, helping another to do likewise.

☐ We must learn how to respect all things Spiritual. The moment we lose respect, we will begin to lose grip of our human psyche. How is this possible, especially when we are an Astute Elite? Frankly, from a Spiritual Perspective, regardless of '*Who*' we are, '*What*' we are, and '*Why*' we are, if we lack respect, behind closed doors, our psyche will grow a bull's eye. The enemy inside of us will take shots at us with negative thoughts, chatter, insecurity, unresolved trauma, or whatever weakness we have, breaking us to the core until we come to ourselves, becoming humbly respectful.

Until then, the inner war will continue, contributing to our fighting against or turning on ourselves. While at the same time, thinking our enemies are all around us, everyone is against us, people are trying to hurt us, and the list goes on with all types of negative deflections. When, in all actuality, everything around us is only responding to us or is caused by our gravitational *pull* from within.

Can all of this happen if we do not develop our *Muscles* according to Kingdom Standards? Absolutely! Without humility and the trainable ability to learn, the Kingdom of Heaven will reject us. Simply put, pompousness comes with disobedience by default, and if we cannot obey, we cannot stay in the Kingdom, period!

Even if we are or pretend to be Heaven Sent, our Spiritual Fruits must represent. If not, the BOOT from the Kingdom will be felt inwardly and not outwardly as most would think. Therefore, we must consistently do a checkup from the neck up with the Fruits of the Spirit while aligning it with Christlike Character to develop our *Kingdom Muscles*.

How do we go from *Mental Muscles*, *Physical Muscles*, *Emotional Muscles*, or *Spiritual Muscles* to *Kingdom Muscles*? We cannot develop our *Kingdom Muscles* without fine-tuning the others first. According to the Heavenly of Heavens, when dealing with the Kingdom, we are a Spiritual Team within ONE.

When we are a part of the ONE, *As It Pleases God*, He will use anything or anyone to help, save, teach, protect, or restore us. Then again, He may outright place us in some form of Spiritual Classroom or Fold, especially when we fall short or become weak, to preserve or reserve us for our Predestined Blueprinted Purpose.

Listen, when Divine Intervention is on our side, we must not take it lightly. We must pay attention. When the Heavens connect directly to us, we cannot afford to miss the call or cue. We must clear our Spiritual Lines or Receptors from all distractions.

Diverted attention is how the enemy gets us to break our focus from the least to the greatest. For this reason, it is important to document or Mind Map our journey. By far, it ensures we can get back on track, especially when the tyrants come out of the woodwork with kryptonite hidden in their pockets, targeting our weaknesses.

How can we avoid the hidden kryptonite designed to break us down? We must develop our *Muscles* from the inside out, allowing nothing or no one to distract us from our God-Given Mission. Just keep in mind that everyone's Divine Blueprint is different. Thus, we must involve the Holy Trinity in the equation to avoid fighting or stressing out over a cup that is not ours in the first place.

What does a cup have to do with anything? It is a symbolic representation of our Spiritual Portion of the Kingdom. If we attempt to participate in a portion, not of our own, there will always be an imbalance within the human psyche, depleting our cup. What does this mean? We will not have peace, allowing chaos, confusion, jealousy, envy, and coveting into our cup or camp.

Disorderly conduct in public or private is not cute on any level, regardless of 'Who' we are, 'Why' we are, or 'What' we are doing. Unbeknown to most, disorderly conduct reveals weakness or Spiritual Unkemptness. Spiritual Unrest is a symbolic indication from the Heavenly of Heavens of being out of order from the inside out. Still, we ignore it just to fit in with the crowd to satiate a vendetta, lust, or longing while drawing us into the Abyss or affecting our Bloodline without us realizing it. How can we avoid this from happening? We must involve the Holy Trinity (The Father, Son, and Holy Spirit) in the equation, use the Fruits of the Spirit, and exhibit Christlike Character in all things.

As a forewarning, if we are using the Name of God to engage in debauchery, hate, evil, disruption, or any form of negativity, we are out of order. How is this possible when we are doing the right thing? In doing right in our own eyes, it does not necessarily make it right in the Eye of God or befitting for the Kingdom. For this reason, we must be careful about what we lay on the doorstep or doorpost of the Kingdom of Heaven.

The Blood of Jesus was the formal sacrifice made for our sacraments, giving us the *Rites of Passage* to the Kingdom. The moment we knowingly or unknowingly misuse or abuse this Divine Right, we must account for it. What does this mean? In the Kingdom, we are expected to exhibit Love, Joy, Peace, Patience, Kindness, Goodness, Faithfulness, Gentleness, and Self-Control to develop Christlike Character, leading the way. Yet, if we contradict what the Kingdom represents without attempting to make the necessary corrections to become better, then our portion becomes bitter, misunderstood, and wishy-washy.

The act of misbehaving does not necessarily imply that an individual is inherently immoral or a bad person. Rather, it is often indicative of a lack of understanding, direction, awareness, or Spiritual Apathy, causing them to become Spiritually Lethargic.

In all reality, or better yet, the truth is, those whom society writes off, rejects, hangs out to dry, or buries while still living are usually the ones with the most extraordinary Spiritual Impact. They can handle shameful rejection more so than the average person. While simultaneously taking a licking and keeping on ticking with their head held high for the Kingdom. How do I know? I was among those who were dismissed and overlooked, camouflaged in plain sight.

For me, being a *Diamond in the Rough* has proven the Spiritual Classroom to be real and effective in bringing forth the Hidden

Sparkle from within. More importantly, it has proven more effective in shining the LIGHT from the Heavenly of Heavens, ILLUMINATING the Spiritual Path for others to follow, *As It Pleases God.*

Are the Divine Effects from the Heavenly Realm real? Absolutely! If one has never experienced Divine Intervention, it could appear like a fairytale or far-fetched. However, once we have a Divine Encounter, we will never doubt it again, regardless of the naysayers, critics, or dream killers. My Battle Scars, *As It Pleased God*, gave me the Spiritual Credentials to converse and write on behalf of the Heavenly of Heavens with outright humility and credence without backing down. For this reason, I am a Spiritual Straight Shooter with hands-on experience.

In seeking the truth from the Realm of the Spirit, we all have this same ability regardless of our past or what others think or feel about us; therefore, excuses are just that...an excuse. So, by putting all of our self-imposed limitations behind us, we must focus on using our *Mental Muscles, Physical Muscles, Emotional Muscles,* or *Spiritual Muscles,* working on ourselves to reverse the negative effects and consequences associated with deterrents from our past.

How can we pinpoint the adverse effects, especially when no one is perfect? Although we are all a work-in-progress, and no one is exempt from the Vicissitudes of Life. Still, if our Bloodline is becoming weak, unfruitful, dilapidated, or easily influenced by the worldly systems of conveyance, we have work to do.

As you flex your *Mental Muscles*, always remember that your *Platform of Greatness* and change begins with you and what you already have in your hand. Here is Moses' Divine Encounter: "So the Lord said to him, 'What is that in your hand?' He said, 'A rod.'" Exodus 4:2. From the Ancient of Days until now, you already possess what you need. USE IT! Once you do, *As It Pleases God*, the Divine Instructions will follow.

Chapter Twelve

PLATFORM OF GREATNESS

Greatness is within all of us; it is built into our DNA, whether we admit, embrace, or deny it. If we do not understand this fact for ourselves, it can lie dormant, suppressing the Creative Genius from within. Our *Platform of Greatness* is more than financial success; it is about being in Purpose on purpose. So, we should never limit ourselves. At some point in our lives, we are going to need something that money cannot buy. When this time avails itself, we must be adequately equipped with the Spiritual Tools to maximize our highest potential, using what we have in hand.

As God Promised, whatever we need is always wrapped in our Gifts, Calling, Talents, Mission, or Creativity; therefore, we must determine a few things, but not limited to such:

- ☐ We must know beyond a shadow of a doubt 'Who' we are and 'Why' we are here.
- ☐ We must know 'What' we are good at, 'What' we are not, and the reasons 'Why.'

- ☐ We must know 'What' drives us, 'What' detours us, the reasons 'Why,' 'How' it affects us, 'Where' it takes place, and with 'Whom.'

The *Spiritual Platform* granted to us when God breathed into us the Breath of Life is by far the most profound reason to maximize our greatest and highest potential. How do we go about doing so? We must begin to use it, documenting our results to become better while training the mind to create a positive, conducive *Win-Win* in our developmental process.

When we develop our agility in using our Gifts, Calling, Talents, and Creativity without any form of shame or reservation, we will find the inner nudging needed to continue the journey toward Greatness. However, we must become aware of our motives at all times, ensuring we are doing things for the right reasons without allowing evil deeds to creep into the crevices of our Mind, Body, and Soul, causing us to secretly or openly turn on ourselves.

According to the Heavenly of Heavens, if we want to become GREAT from the inside out, we must begin to extract it by skillfully choosing the positive. At the same time, learning how to deflate or flip the script on the negative to elevate the Platform of the Kingdom. What about our personal platform? The moment we begin to stand for the Righteousness of the Kingdom, our *Platform of Greatness* begins the building process from the ground up with various levels of charactorial training.

Why do we need charactorial training? If our character is not built from the inside out, we will subconsciously build from the outside in with worldly simulations, causing us to collapse or react under pressure, especially when we cannot have our way.

Unbeknown to most, our *Platform of Greatness* is a compilation of our inner experiences turned into a positive outward manifestation. What does this mean? We must extract the positive of whatever is going on from within by learning, understanding, and redirecting the negative to create a *Win-Win*.

How do we go about extracting to create *Win-Wins*? It is best done through asking ourselves fact-finding questions in the form of *What, When, Where, How, Why*, and with *Whom*, while honestly documenting the answers. For example, if someone hurts us, we find a way to ask many questions to better understand their reasoning, right? So, when dealing with ourselves, we are no different. We must get into the habit of questioning ourselves to ensure we do not become our worst enemy or cause our people skills to become repulsive and abrasive.

Truthfully, we all have had good intentions turn bad, and vice versa. However, when dealing with our *Platform of Greatness*, we must become consistent, primarily when representing the Kingdom of Heaven.

Nevertheless, when extracting information from ourselves or when self-analysis occurs, it is perfectly okay and expected for negativity to appear. Still, it is our responsibility to dig deep within our psyche, find the root cause, and then reverse it into a positive. Why do we need to unearth negativity? When operating without a conscience, the Spirit of God cannot remain!

Why is positive consistency necessary? Our responsibility is to fine-tune ways to overcome the negative darts designed to disrupt our Kingdom Consistency. When we are wishy-washy or doubtful, we are easily swayed into anything, especially when there is some form of benefit involved. Yet, the true *Platform of Greatness*, according to the Heavenly of Heavens, is a non-compromising zone of Divine Relations.

Amid doing our due diligence, if God allows a negative penetration to form against us, there is a Blessing, a Lesson, Information, Training, or Revelation attached. *Spirit to Spirit*, we must find a way around, through, over, or under, leaving no stone unturned, documenting our findings of the *Win-Win* as a Testament or Testimony. What if we leave no stone unturned, and it does not yield? Listen to me, and listen well; every stone tilled has something to offer, especially when our motives are righteous. We may have to dig deep, searching for it, but it will yield the answer, especially if we put a Spiritual Demand on it.

Suppose we are not well-versed in this process or want to cut through the distracting hogwash. *As It Pleases God*, it is best to align our stone or our thorn in the flesh with the Word of God while developing a Plan of Action. Once done, then apply the Fruits of the Spirit, perfecting our God-Game to make sure all is well within us, *As It Pleases Him*.

Is our Plan of Action the same as a Mind Map? No, they are similar but different, working together to achieve a common goal. When doing a POA (Plan of Action) for the Win-Win, we must:

- ☐ Write down our Goal, Desire, or Vision in one or two sentences. A brief synopsis is needed in the first step.
- ☐ Ask our Goal, Desire, or Vision fact-finding questions in the *What, When, Where, How, Why*, and with *Whom* Formation. Doing so helps us extract the pertinent information needed in the next step.
- ☐ We should paint a visual *Mental Picture* of our Goal, Desire, or Vision in detailed documentation. We can use Mind Mapping to help us paint a visual picture, but we must document this Mental Presentation so that someone else can fully understand what we ENVISION. If we are the only ones who can *Mentally See* the Vision, we must go back to the Drawing Board. To be clear, no one has to agree with our Vision, but according to the Heavenly of Heavens, they must be able to understand and follow along with their Mind's Eye.
- ☐ Then, we must take the whole Vision and divide it into a step-by-step process. Once we build the Vision, we must then break it down one step at a time. Doing so develops our Mental Mindset into creating a Systematic Process of creating subdivisions. Compartmentalizing our Visions or Goals helps narrow down which areas need more or less development, and this is where Mind Mapping comes into full play. When developing a Plan of Action, our step-by-step process should never match another person's process; here is a sample:

As It Pleases God: Book Series

THE WIN-WIN OF GREATNESS
Plan of Action

What: (What is the Goal, Desire, or Vision?)

When: (When do we plan for the Vision to take place?)

Where: (Where will this Vision take place?)

How: (How does one plan to achieve the Vision?)

Why: (Why is this Vision so important?)

Whom: (Who is required or needed in this Vision?)

THE WIN-WIN OF DIVINE GREATNESS

Paint The Mental Picture

THE WIN-WIN OF DIVINE GREATNESS

Step-By-Step Process

Once again, we all have a unique Blueprint; therefore, what is coming from our Gifts, Calling, Talents, Creativity, or Purpose should NOT match another. There may be similarities, but a replica is not a part of *The Win-Win of Divine Greatness*. In the same way that we have a different finger, eye, or footprint, our Plan of Action should take on this form of authenticity. What if we have a problem painting a mental picture? We must practice.

If it is challenging to document our Goals, Desires, or Visions, it is okay. We only need to calm down the inner chatter while taking one step at a time. I promise it will begin to flow, especially if the instructions in this book are followed accordingly. Plus, it does not matter how many times we have to redo or revamp our POA or Mind Map; practice, consistency, and patience make our good better, better to best, and best to Greatest.

After we document our findings, we present our case privately to the Holy Trinity (The Father, Son, and Holy Spirit) in a state of transparency and repentance. Once our case is presented in the Realm of the Spirit, we must exhibit Christlike Character in all of our endeavors, using the Fruits of the Spirit as corrective measures while still documenting our daily findings. After doing so, or when getting the ball rolling on our transparency, we need to do a Mind Map, documenting the information given as it relates to each unyielding stone, the thorn in our flesh, or our Divine Blueprint. Each unyielding stone or thorn has Divine Wisdom attached to our Divine Blueprint, and we must learn how to extract, convert, manifest, and share it.

How is it possible to extract, manifest, and share when we are clueless? First and foremost, just because we feel clueless does not mean we are. If we know our likes and dislikes, we have a platform to work with. Once again, the key to all things is asking ourselves fact-finding questions in the form of *What, When, Where, How, Why*, and with *Whom*, and then documenting our answers without being distracted by worldliness. Once we gain Spiritual Insight regarding whatever or whomever, we are better able to grow, sow, and do more in the Kingdom.

As It Pleases God: Book Series

In *The Win-Win of Divine Greatness*, when availing ourselves to using the Fruits of the Spirit and Christlike Character in our *Plan of Action*, we must do a few things, but not limited to such:

- ☐ We must effectively listen.
- ☐ We must willfully learn.
- ☐ We must clearly understand.
- ☐ We must intuitively obey.
- ☐ We must naturally grow.
- ☐ We must cheerfully sow.
- ☐ We must undoubtedly articulate.
- ☐ We must consciously relate.
- ☐ We must compassionately communicate.
- ☐ We must studiously document, document, document.
- ☐ We must proactively pay attention from the inside out.
- ☐ We must thankfully put the Holy Trinity at the forefront of all things.

What is the purpose of doing this when developing a POA? It helps us to build Spiritual Empathy and Awareness, making us Spiritually Sensitive. We have better results when we are Spiritually Sensitive as opposed to using our worldly senses.

To be clear, we can do and accomplish incredible feats outside of using Spirituality; however, if we are accomplishing things that take us outside of our Divine Blueprint, we will still become unsatisfied or experience a void from within. Spiritually Speaking, if we incorporate our Divine Blueprint in the *Win-Win*, we waste less time undoing, redoing, and subduing; instead, we can Spiritually Envision the Vision, Empower the Plan, and Encourage others to do likewise.

When we become Spirit-Led, the Holy Spirit will give us Spiritual Cues and Clues, guiding us to the Light of our Divine Blueprint or the Kingdom. If we pay attention to our ability to recognize, connect, and master, He will not miss a beat. On the other hand, if a beat is missed, we must quickly recalibrate or recalculate our erring process, correcting the correctable. Yet, with our POA and Mind Map, we can quickly pinpoint where the beat was missed and target the *Win-Win*, especially if they are precise and organized.

Amid gaining Spiritual Insight, we still must Spiritually Till our own ground with our Gifts, Calling, Talents, Purpose, and Creativity in hand without dropping the ball. In the Kingdom, we must put in the work because the *Platform of Greatness* will not fall into our laps. We must Step Up, Grow Up, Level Up, Turn Up, and Wise Up, *As It Pleases God*! What is the purpose of going through all of this? Most often, when it comes down to *Greatness*, we tend to fall short due to the lack of understanding or the inability to truthfully engage in a *Q and A Session* with ourselves.

For example, I recognize the level of *Greatness* in someone by the way they pay attention, ask questions, document answers, and find solutions. What about the good fruits or character? They play a dynamic role in our *Platform of Greatness*, but if we cannot put in the work, document instructions, ask the right questions, and so on, we become limited, especially in the Kingdom.

Keep in mind that good fruits and character are trainable, but they do not stop fear, negativity, and the wiles of the enemy. Nor do they teach us how to use the Word of God as a Weapon of Spiritual Warfare; therefore, we must put in the work, *As It Pleases God*, while using the Holy Spirit and covering ourselves with the Blood of Jesus.

Are good fruits or character the same as Spiritual Fruits and Christlike Character? No, they are totally different. A worldly system teaches one, and the other is from a Spiritual System. From a Heavenly Perspective, this is where the two systems are colliding! We are trying to make them one when they are NOT designed as such. For this reason, we must incorporate the Holy Trinity (The Father, Son, and Holy Spirit) in all things. By far, it gives us the Unction to Function according to Kingdom Standards, going above and beyond the worldly system of operation. What does this mean? The *Platform of Greatness* in the worldly system is totally different from the Spiritual Expectations set forth by God from the beginning of our existence.

The Divine Wisdom from the Heavenly of Heavens is written on the tablet of the heart beneath layers of debris, and we need the Holy Spirit to decode for us. Is this Biblical? I would have it no other way! *"But the Helper, the Holy Spirit, whom the Father will send in My name, He will teach you all things, and bring to your remembrance all things that I said to you."* John 14:26. Simply put, the Holy Spirit will decode what is already within us according to our Predestined Blueprint, and He will not mislead us.

To maximize our *Platform of Greatness*, we must balance it between our Mind, Body, and Soul, building consistency. How is this possible when faced with the Vicissitudes of Life? To avoid having the *Mind* say one thing and our *Body* do another. We need to involve the Holy Spirit to tame our *Soulish* nature while covering ourselves with the Blood of Jesus and using the Word of God as our point of reference or Spiritual Sword.

What can the Word of God do for us? It gives us Spiritual Leverage to quote back to God, confirming or Spiritually Sealing whatever we are dealing with according to the Spiritual Laws, Principles, and Concepts set forth. Does it work? Of course, it does. Frankly, if it did not, one would not be reading one of *His Promises* right now!

On the other hand, if we are praying without the Word of God backing it up, we are most often praying amiss. Personally, I have been around long enough to hear a few heartfelt prayers violating the will of another, creating generational curses, asking God to bring harm to another, selfishly coveting, or engaging in treacherous debauchery without any form of repentance, thanksgiving, reverence, or fix me, O' Lord.

When dealing with our *Platform of Greatness*, before praying about anything, it is best to find the scriptures associated with the issue, ask for the presence and guidance of the Holy Spirit, and cover the prayer with the Blood of Jesus or in the Name of Jesus. To ensure we do not unawaringly dethrone ourselves, intending to do the right thing, yet wrong according to the Heavenly of

Heavens. Can this really happen? It happens all the time; we often do not realize what is happening until the deed is done or the generational curse is set in motion.

Unfortunately, when we pray against someone amissly or without just cause, we will have that same character trait show up in someone we love. It is often within the weakest link, which happens to be with our children, tainting our Bloodline. For this reason, it is best to approach our prayers by working on ourselves first, cleaning our Spiritual House (Our Temple), and then spreading outwardly to make a positive impact.

The moment we find ourselves all over the place, becoming a little sketchy, skittish, or tossed to and fro, we must hone in on the Principles of Wisdom. Our *Platform of Greatness* is under attack, and if we stay under the covering of our Divine Purpose, God will protect what belongs to Him. What does this mean for us? If we are on God's watch, He governs what takes place during the time we remain in Purpose on purpose. On the other hand, if we are defiant and out of Divine Purpose on purpose, we are on our own until we come to ourselves, *As It Pleases Him.*

How do we make this make sense, especially when grace is on our side as Believers? If we choose to selfishly or piously do our own thing or the wrong thing, we forfeit our Divine Covering held under our Divine Blueprint. Unfortunately, it will remain until we make a conscious effort to restore it or AWAKEN the Holy Spirit to take the wheel of our misdirection.

Clearly, no one is exempt from this process, and we are all a work-in-progress; however, we must understand the value of our Divine Covering and restoring ourselves at the drop of a dime. How do we restore ourselves? Listed below are a few ways, but not limited to such:

- ☐ Ask for Divine Intervention or Understanding from the Holy Trinity.
- ☐ Repent of all negativity involved with the lust of the flesh, the lust of the eyes, and the pride of life.
- ☐ Replace or counteract all negative self-talk with positive affirmations.

- ☐ Ask fact-finding questions to ensure our positive or negative triggers do not become our kryptonite.
- ☐ Document the lessons, answers, or thoughts associated.
- ☐ Practice, focus, or work toward positive betterment daily.
- ☐ Do not make excuses.
- ☐ We must own and properly articulate our truth without suppressing it or expressing it irresponsibly, disrespectfully, or untimely.
- ☐ Give thanks in all things, the good, bad, or indifferent.
- ☐ Determine our *'Give-Back'* to the Kingdom.
- ☐ Tame the inner chatter while making sure it Spiritually Affirms what the Kingdom of Heaven has in mind according to our Divine Blueprint.
- ☐ Properly govern the GATEWAY of our Mind, Body, Soul, and Spirit.

When dealing with our *Platform of Greatness*, keep in mind that we are all different. So, what works for one person could be child's play or *Spiritual Milk* for the next, depending upon our Spiritual Status. Still, we should never discount a step in bridging the gap between our *Spiritual Meat* and *Divine Access* to the Kingdom.

According to the Heavenly of Heavens, our Mental, Physical, Emotional, and Spiritual habits determine the stability of our *Spiritual Platform*. From my perspective, what we put on our plate forms us. What does this mean? Our *Platform of Greatness* is determined by what we knowingly or unknowingly put on our plate, in our cup, or what we consume Mentally, Physically, Emotionally, and Spiritually. It determines our Kingdom Formation or worldly deformational status.

To be clear, I am not judging. I am only bringing awareness to the fact that we decide on the type of platform given. Listed below are a few versus examples, but not limited to such:

- ☐ A *Platform of Greatness* vs. a platform of failure.
- ☐ A *Platform of Strength* vs. a platform of weakness.

- ☐ A *Platform of Love* vs. a platform of hate.
- ☐ A *Platform of Responsibility* vs. a platform of recklessness.
- ☐ A *Platform of Sustainability* vs. a platform of drought.
- ☐ A *Platform of Blessings* vs. a platform of curses.
- ☐ A *Platform of Opportunities* vs. a platform of stumbling blocks.
- ☐ A *Platform of Respect* vs. a platform of contempt.
- ☐ A *Platform of Selflessness* vs. a platform of self-centeredness.
- ☐ A *Platform of Integrity* vs. a platform of disgrace.
- ☐ A *Platform of Truth* vs. a platform of deception.
- ☐ A *Platform of Righteousness* vs. a platform of injustice.

Here is the deal: Our present conscious or unconscious platform does not determine our future platforms unless we choose NOT to do anything about it while refusing to correct the correctable.

God will use anyone or anything to accomplish His Divine Purpose as long as we do our part. So, regardless of our background, mistakes, conditioning, or whatever, we can become usable, especially if we are genuinely REPENTING. In addition, we must become WILLING to grow through the Spiritual Transformational process to top the charts with our *Platform of Greatness*.

When it comes down to the Kingdom of Heaven, the '*Cream Of The Crop*' will always rise to the top in due time, but we must not give up on ourselves. Most importantly, we cannot give up on God. Most often, when we think we are ready, we are NOT according to Kingdom Standards. The pruning process is just as challenging as being in a holding pattern; however, we must understand that the timing must be right as well.

When dealing with our *Platform of Greatness*, doing something at the wrong time or in the incorrect season creates a disservice in the Kingdom. What does inappropriate timing have to do with the Kingdom? When our timing is off, it means we are not properly synced to the Kingdom, and the Holy Spirit is lying dormant or standing down for a reason.

According to the Heavenly of Heavens, when we are always a day late and a dollar short, we need a checkup from the neck up. We must evaluate our underlying motives or take ourselves into the Spiritual Classroom to pinpoint our secret or open kryptonic ailments. Yet, when doing so, we must make sure we are documenting accordingly.

Why must we document? Over a period of time, we tend to forget some of the lessons learned. For example, when we keep repeating ourselves to someone who refuses to document or pay attention, we feel as if the person is behaving defiantly or negligently. The same applies to Kingdom Formality; in short, to avoid repeating the process or wasting time, it is reverential to take notes, similar to the Disciples documenting their accounts with Jesus. Plus, when we have our notes to reflect on or build upon, our Spiritual Platform becomes stronger. As a whole, we become more equipped to endure the Vicissitudes of Life without becoming blown away, beaten down, or panicky.

As we all know, obstacles will come, and they will also go; it is just a matter of time. Amid all, we must remember they are opportunities hidden in plain sight; therefore, if we properly dissect them to extract the *Win-Win*, we will find the Spirit of Wisdom will call our name, placing us at the forefront of the Divine Stream. What does this mean? We are the Tree of Life, bringing life to another to continue the Spiritual Cycle with our *Platform of Greatness*.

If we digress in the formality of our Divine Blueprint, refusing to be in Purpose on purpose, we become the Tree of Death by default. Blasphemy, right? Wrong! As gruesome as it seems, the Cycle of Life is designed to take out the weak, unfruitful, or damaged. And we are no different!

I do not wish doom and gloom on anyone, so please allow me to align this with scripture. *"He shall be like a tree Planted by the rivers of water, that brings forth its fruit in its season, whose leaf also shall not wither; and whatever he does shall prosper. The ungodly are not so, but are like the chaff which the wind drives away. Therefore the ungodly shall not stand in the judgment, nor sinners in the congregation of the righteous. For the LORD knows the way of the righteous, but the way of the ungodly shall perish."* Psalm 1:3-6.

For us, in Earthen Vessels, the cycle of death begins within the human psyche as a void, longing, thirst, hunger, and so on. Having these feelings will not make us a bad person; it is only an indication that we must make a conscious choice to reverse the cycle. How so? It begins with us AWAKENING our Spirit to become ONE with the Holy Spirit while becoming happily content with who God created us to be.

Our *Platform of Greatness* can also be found in our *Weapon of Happiness*. Our ability to happily look for the *Win-Win* in all things is a valuable skill to master, bringing our Heavenly Impact to earthly. Unbeknown to most, this state of being is a choice we make for ourselves based on outside circumstances or conditions. What does this mean? In the same way that we choose to be unhappy about something or someone, it takes the same amount of energy or less to become happy by changing our mindset. Although the Vicissitudes of Life may be unavoidable, it does not mean we have to succumb to its effects.

How can we avoid becoming a victim of unhappiness? We must become *Grateful* in all things, giving *Thanks* even if it does not appear as if we should be THANKFUL, do it anyway. Why? First and foremost, hate festers negativity within the human psyche. Secondly, most of our Blessings are hidden in a problem that appears real based on our perception. The moment we begin to maximize our ability to reverse negatives into positives, we will find our inner-born counterbalancing system stepping into high gear, canceling out or avoiding disruptive rudimentary factors associated with foolery.

In today's day and age, this Spiritual Principle is similar to having virus protection to safeguard our computers. If we do not protect ourselves, we become vulnerable to anything from anywhere and anyone.

Comprised in the Elements of Happiness lies one characteristic we overlook, but is necessary in our *Platform of Greatness*. What is it? Cheerfulness! *"A merry heart makes a cheerful countenance, but by sorrow of the heart the spirit is broken."* Proverbs 15:13. Therefore, if we work on our Cheerful Countenance, we will find it sparks our inner joyfulness by default as it protects it from the worldly zaps of negativity.

What does Cheerfulness have to do with our *Platform of Greatness*? Let me counteract this question with another: 'How Great are we if we do not feel great?' My point exactly! We cannot enjoy our Platform if we are sad, depressed, or feeling unworthy. For this reason, we must get a little spark going on from the inside out. What is the purpose of doing so? In the Kingdom, we must incorporate this in our *'Give-Back.'*

Most of us attempt to associate our *'Give-Back'* with money. Well, today, I am putting an end to this thwarted misconception. Frankly, this is how deception runs rampant among Believers, tricking us. When giving *Spirit to Spirit*, we must avoid transferring negativity or evil when doing so, especially when using our Gifts, Calling, Talents, Purpose, or Creativity. Is this Biblical? I would have it no other way. *"So let each one give as he purposes in his heart, not grudgingly or of necessity; for God loves a cheerful giver. And God is able to make all grace abound toward you, that you, always having all sufficiency in all things, may have an abundance for every good work."* 2 Corinthians 9:7-8. The keywords here are *In All Things* and *Every Good Work!*

When dealing with our *Platform of Greatness*, everything we give, say, and do is a manifestation of positive or negative energy, from the tangible to the intangible. To emphasize further, we must become AWARE of what we are setting in motion on a moment-by-moment basis.

Our *Weapon of Cheerfulness* is associated with making outwardly joyful noises, such as positive speaking, singing, worshiping, sounds, and so on. In addition, it is also connected inwardly to smiling as well. Unbeknown to most, it is hard to remain mad, sad, or depressed when we smile or laugh with good energy. Besides, if we desire to break negative tension, find a way to get the person on the opposite end to laugh or smile. It gives us time to reverse the negativity into a *Win-Win* or break the ice.

When we smile a lot, the enemy will think we are weak and giggly. But in all actuality, it is our Hidden Power, harnessed for the right time. Here is what Proverbs 17:1 says: "*A merry heart does good, like medicine, but a broken spirit dries the bones.*" Joyfulness is MEDICINE for our inner man, and if we do not take our doses of Cheerfulness, we can become dried out, brittle, and broken.

Clearly, I am not saying we should use laughter as a form of mockery, similar to what the scripture describes as a menace; it says, "*If the scourge slays suddenly, He laughs at the plight of the innocent.*" Job 9:23. In the Kingdom, this behavior is greatly frowned upon.

Nevertheless, when our enemy is pouncing upon us, it is in our nature to respond negatively; however, in the Kingdom, when we respond positively with a smile, it gives us Spiritual Leverage to call for Heavenly Backup at the drop of a dime.

Regardless of what we are going through or why, we must govern our countenance accordingly. Here is a scripture that floored and empowered me beyond measure. "*And Hannah prayed and said: 'My heart rejoices in the LORD; my horn is exalted in the LORD. I smile at my enemies, because I rejoice in Your salvation. No one is holy like the LORD, for there is none besides You, nor is there any rock like our God.' Talk no more so very proudly; let no arrogance come from your mouth, for the LORD is the God of knowledge; and by Him actions are weighed.*" 1 Samuel 2:1-3.

When we can humbly smile at our enemies, bearing no grudges, we will know God is doing a good work within us, *As It Pleases Him*. Thus, no one can circumvent our Joy, Happiness, or Cheerfulness without our participation.

In Recognizing, Connecting, and Mastering our Divine Destiny or Blueprint, the Power and Presence of God have provided the Spiritual Tools needed for the Restoration Process from this point onward. All we need to do is pinpoint the missing links, connect the dots, and create a *Win-Win* approach, elevating ourselves to the next level in a State of Fullness in Christ Jesus.

From one recipient to another, we are not alone; the Lord of all is in us all, awaiting the *Spirit to Spirit* Connection to download our Heavenly Instructions. If one has made it to this point in the '*As It*

Pleases God' Book Collection without deviation, and with a commitment to the Holy Trinity, the unveiling of Divine Secrets, Mysteries, Wisdom, Revelation, Understanding, and the Spiritual Classroom are at their beck and call.

According to the Ancients of Ancients, if we refuse to settle for negative mediocrity, we inadvertently empower ourselves with Seeds of Faith, building and taking us where we could not go otherwise. Moreover, a Kingdom Approach keeps us rooted and grounded with stability to maintain and sustain whatever and with whomever as we take the next step upward, *As It Pleases God*. Now, with this in mind, the engrafted step-by-step process in our *Spirit to Spirit* Journey can be made at our own pace from the least to the GREATEST, leaving no stone unturned, especially when searching for *The Win-Win of Divine Greatness*.

In Conclusion, it does not matter what you have done or what you have been through; you are still usable if you are willing to become used by God according to His Will and Ways. Once again, I believe in you! No matter what you see with your naked eyes, you have what it takes! So, fix your HEART and MIND, follow the instructions given, and do what you have been called to do for the Kingdom. Grow Great and Many Blessings.

Dr. Y. Bur

As It Pleases God: Book Series

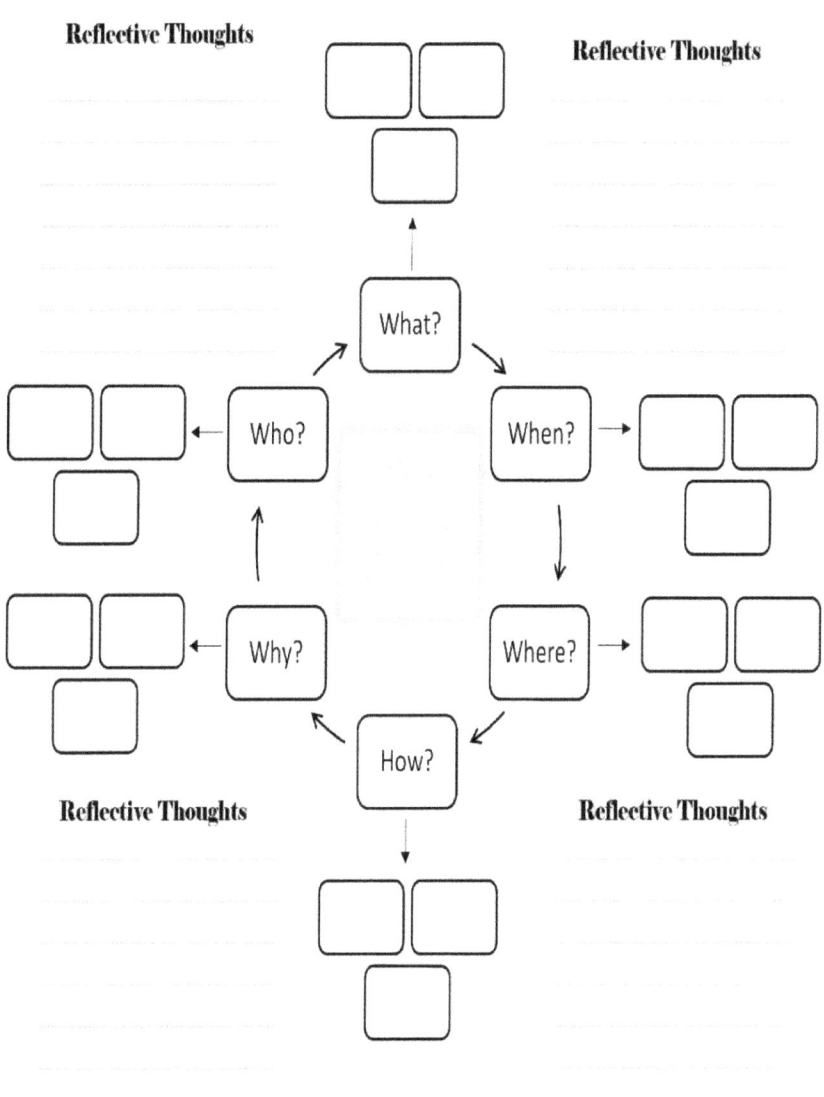

WHAT IS YOUR TAKE-AWAY OR ULTIMATE ACHIEVEMENT?

As It Pleases God: Book Series

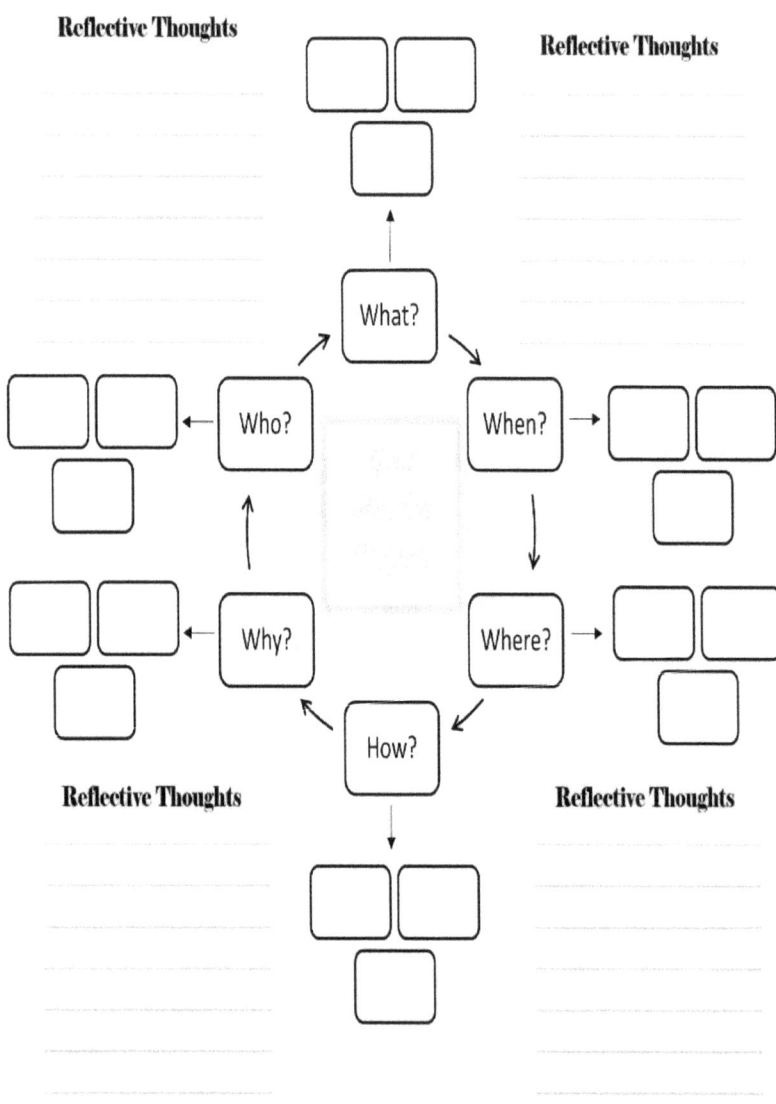

WHAT IS YOUR TAKE-AWAY OR ULTIMATE ACHIEVEMENT?

As It Pleases God: Book Series

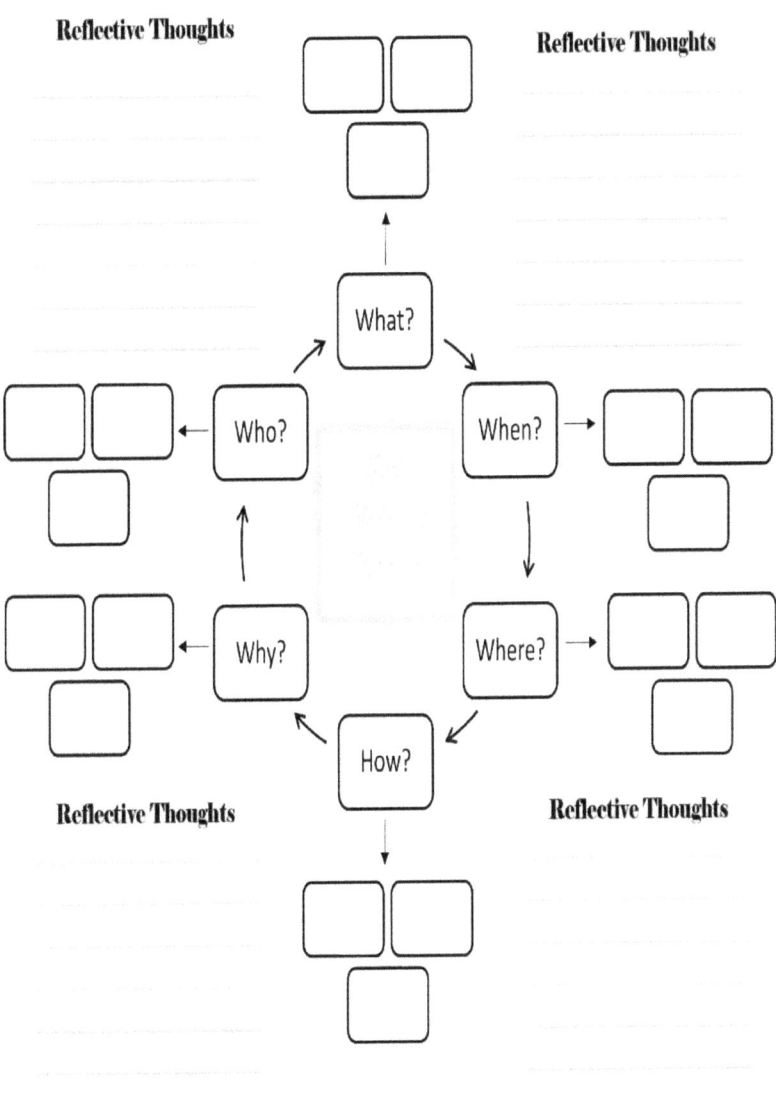

WHAT IS YOUR TAKE-AWAY OR ULTIMATE ACHIEVEMENT?

As It Pleases God: Book Series

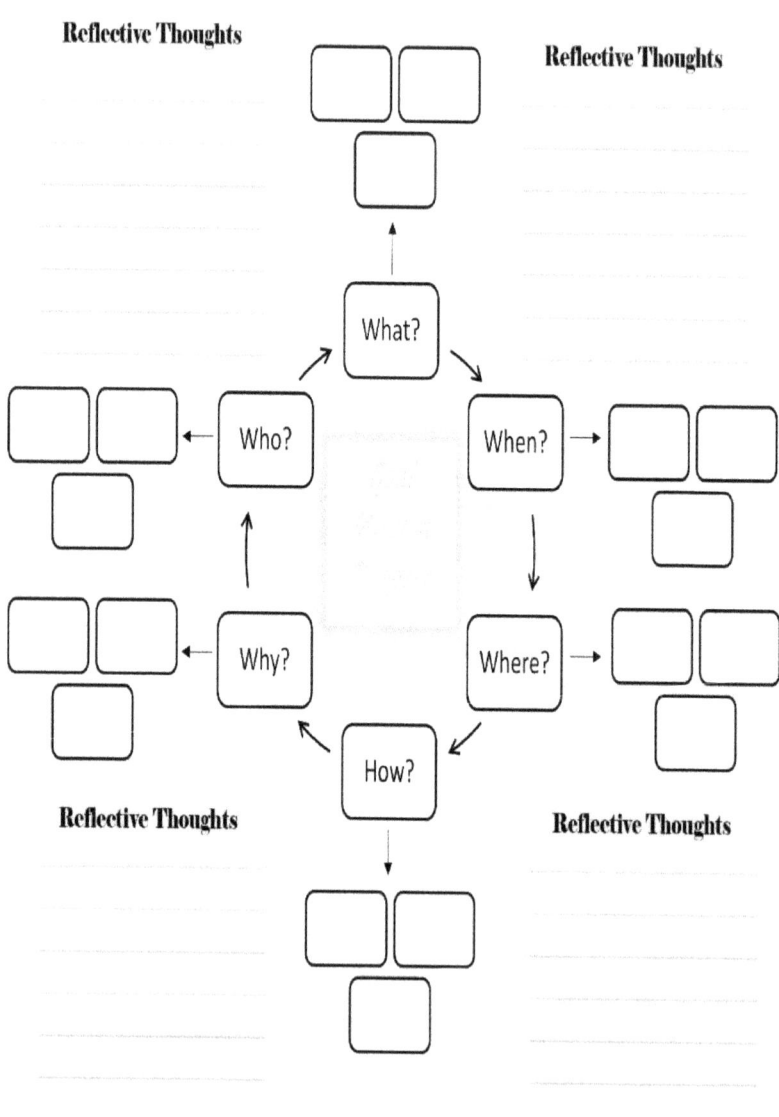

WHAT IS YOUR TAKE-AWAY OR ULTIMATE ACHIEVEMENT?

As It Pleases God: Book Series

THE WIN-WIN OF GREATNESS
Plan of Action

What: (What is the Goal, Desire, or Vision?)

When: (When do we plan for the Vision to take place?)

Where: (Where will this Vision take place?)

How: (How does one plan to achieve the Vision?)

Why: (Why is this Vision so important?)

Whom: (Who is required or needed in this Vision?)

THE WIN-WIN OF DIVINE GREATNESS
Paint The Mental Picture

THE WIN-WIN OF DIVINE GREATNESS

Step-By-Step Process

As It Pleases God: Book Series

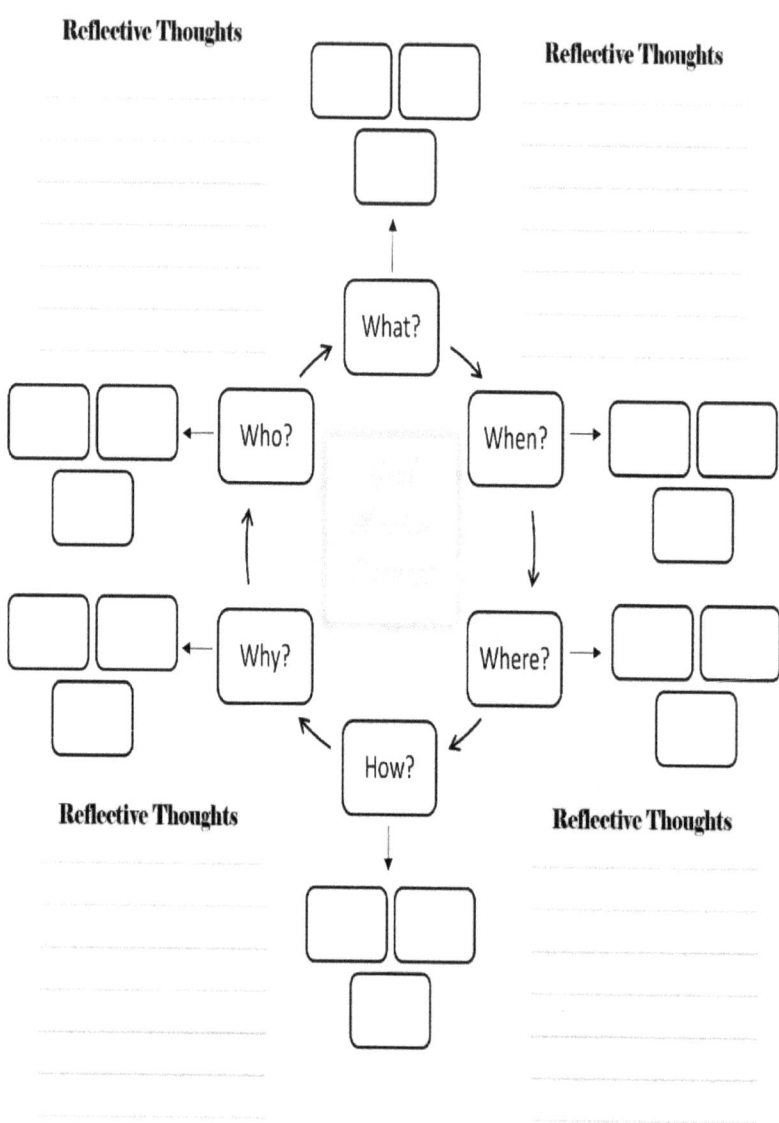

WHAT IS YOUR TAKE-AWAY OR ULTIMATE ACHIEVEMENT?

As It Pleases God: Book Series

THE WIN-WIN OF GREATNESS
Plan of Action

What: (What is the Goal, Desire, or Vision?)

When: (When do we plan for the Vision to take place?)

Where: (Where will this Vision take place?)

How: (How does one plan to achieve the Vision?)

Why: (Why is this Vision so important?)

Whom: (Who is required or needed in this Vision?)

THE WIN-WIN OF DIVINE GREATNESS

Paint The Mental Picture

THE WIN-WIN OF DIVINE GREATNESS

Step-By-Step Process

As It Pleases God: Book Series

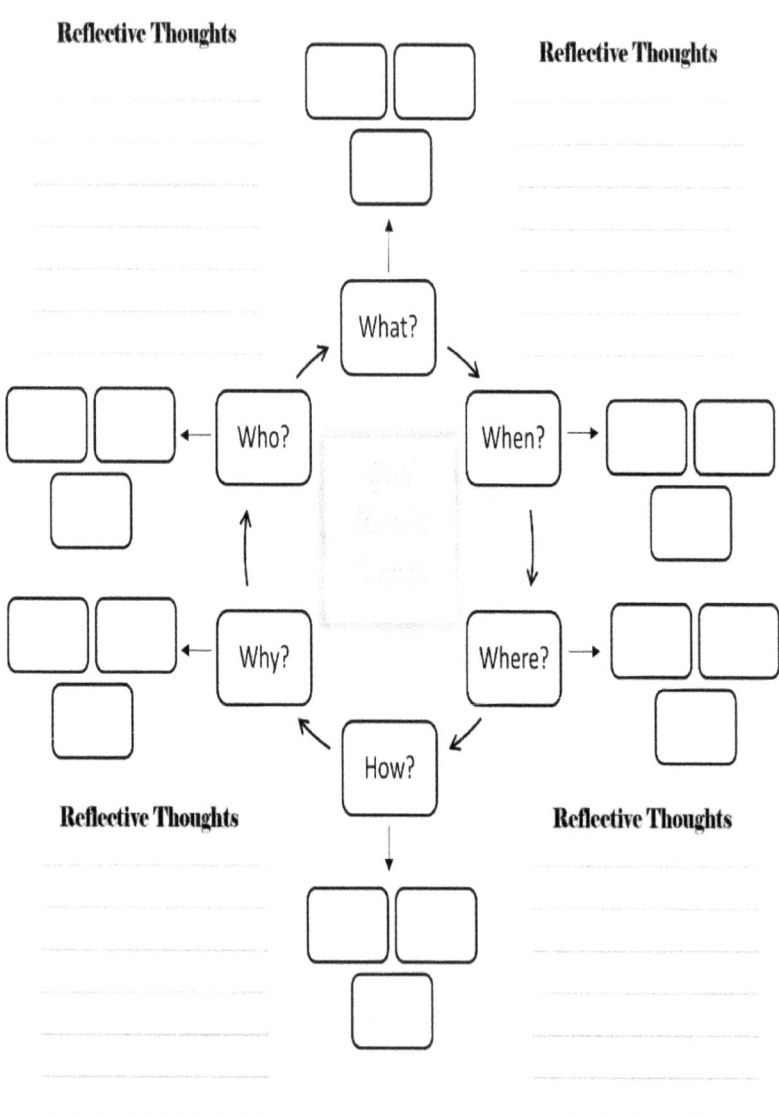

WHAT IS YOUR TAKE-AWAY OR ULTIMATE ACHIEVEMENT?

As It Pleases God: Book Series

THE WIN-WIN OF GREATNESS
Plan of Action

What: (What is the Goal, Desire, or Vision?)

When: (When do we plan for the Vision to take place?)

Where: (Where will this Vision take place?)

How: (How does one plan to achieve the Vision?)

Why: (Why is this Vision so important?)

Whom: (Who is required or needed in this Vision?)

As It Pleases God: Book Series

THE WIN-WIN OF DIVINE GREATNESS

Paint The Mental Picture

THE WIN-WIN OF DIVINE GREATNESS

Step-By-Step Process

As It Pleases God: Book Series

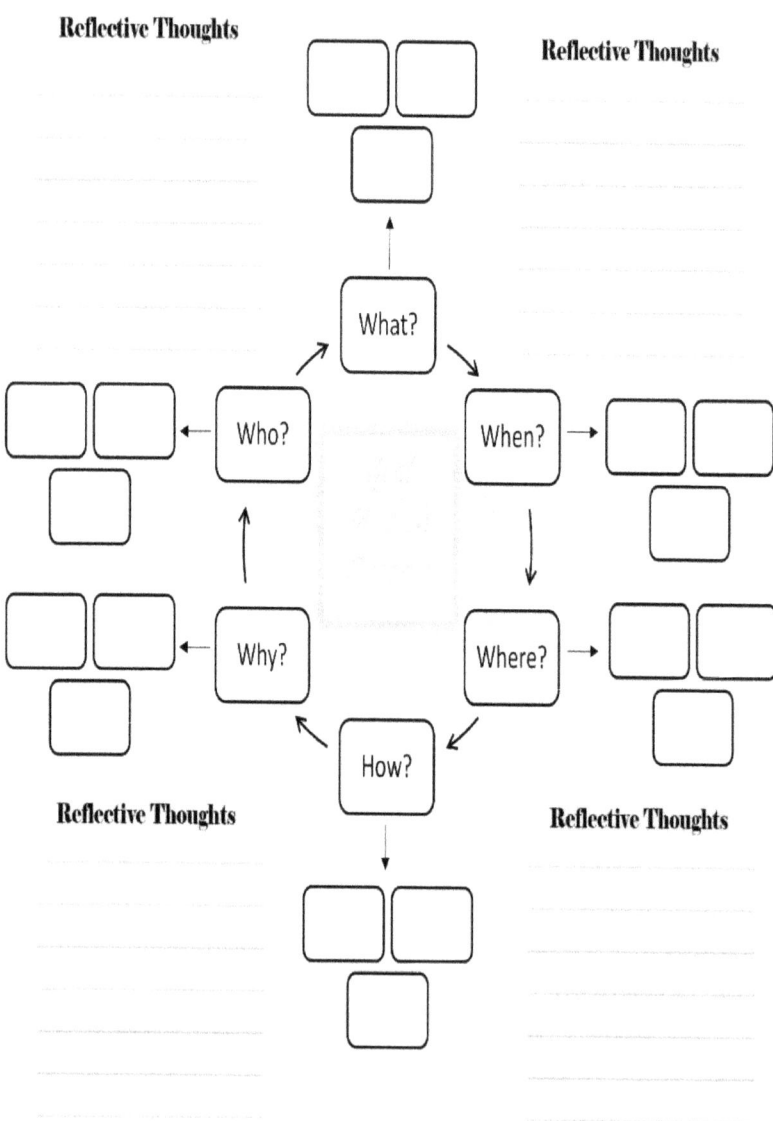

WHAT IS YOUR TAKE-AWAY OR ULTIMATE ACHIEVEMENT?

As It Pleases God: Book Series

THE WIN-WIN OF GREATNESS
Plan of Action

What: (What is the Goal, Desire, or Vision?)

When: (When do we plan for the Vision to take place?)

Where: (Where will this Vision take place?)

How: (How does one plan to achieve the Vision?)

Why: (Why is this Vision so important?)

Whom: (Who is required or needed in this Vision?)

As It Pleases God: Book Series

THE WIN-WIN OF DIVINE GREATNESS

Paint The Mental Picture

THE WIN-WIN OF DIVINE GREATNESS

Step-By-Step Process

As It Pleases God: Book Series

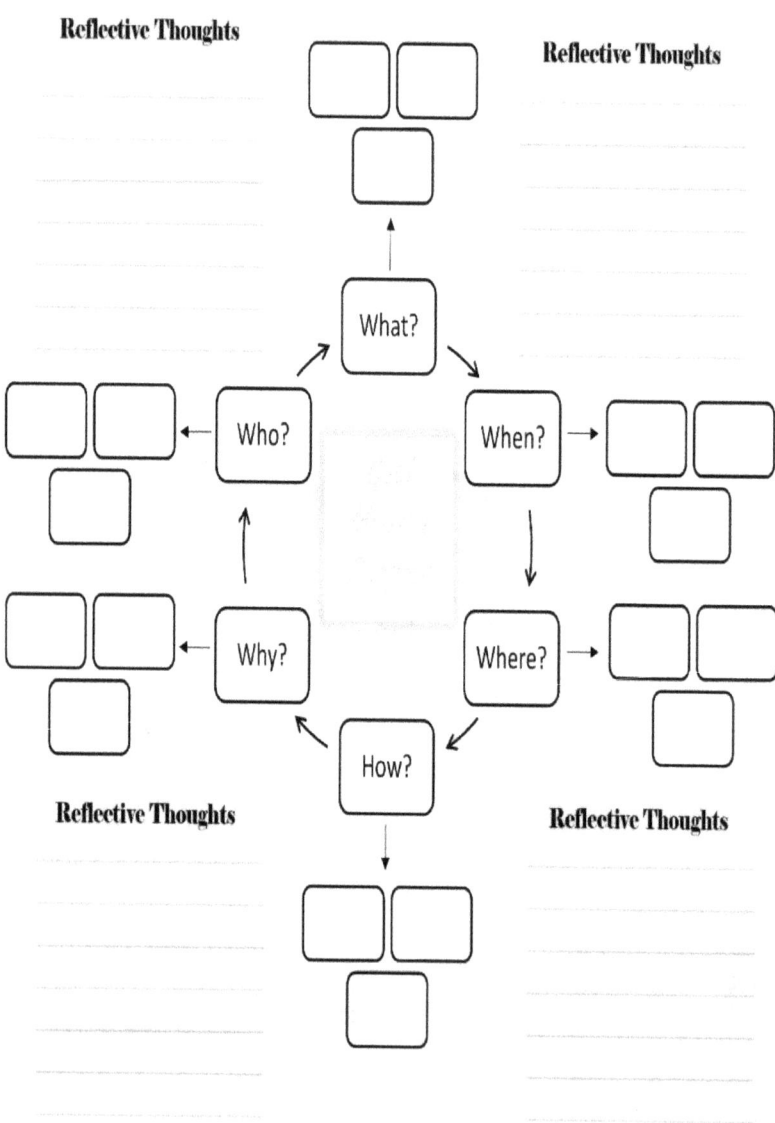

WHAT IS YOUR TAKE-AWAY OR ULTIMATE ACHIEVEMENT?

THE WIN-WIN OF GREATNESS
Plan of Action

What: (What is the Goal, Desire, or Vision?)

When: (When do we plan for the Vision to take place?)

Where: (Where will this Vision take place?)

How: (How does one plan to achieve the Vision?)

Why: (Why is this Vision so important?)

Whom: (Who is required or needed in this Vision?)

As It Pleases God: Book Series

THE WIN-WIN OF DIVINE GREATNESS

Paint The Mental Picture

THE WIN-WIN OF DIVINE GREATNESS

Step-By-Step Process

As It Pleases God: Book Series

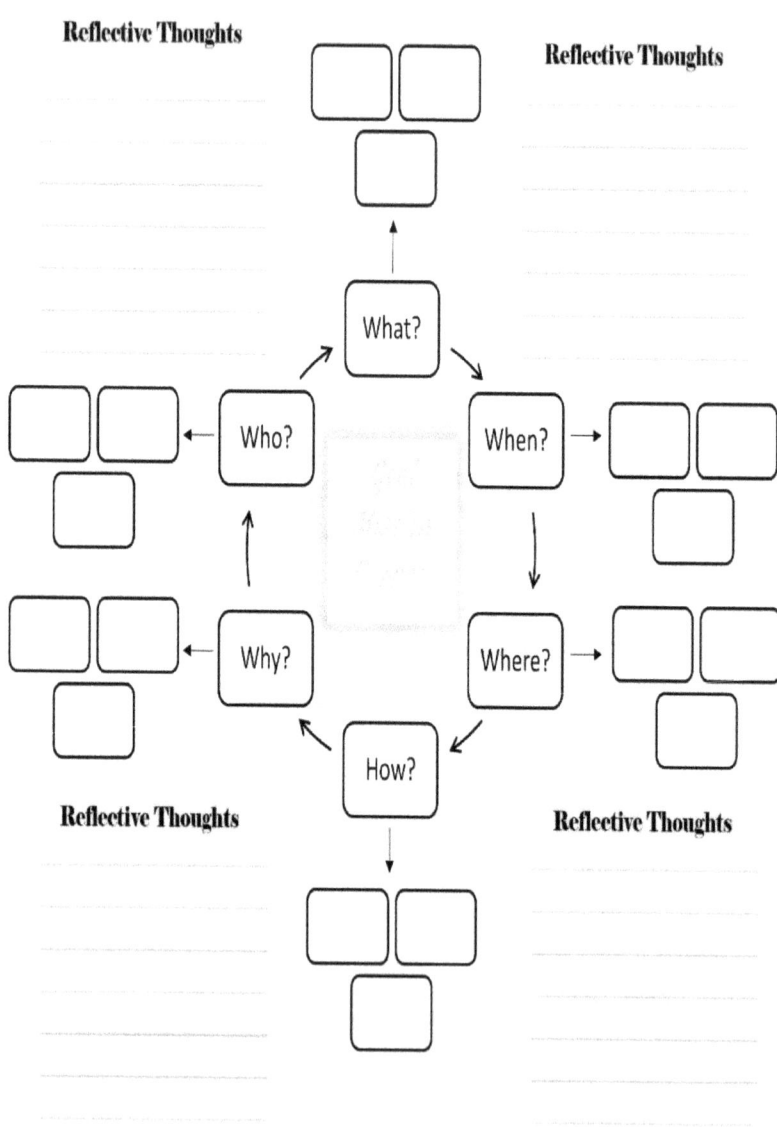

WHAT IS YOUR TAKE-AWAY OR ULTIMATE ACHIEVEMENT?

www.ingramcontent.com/pod-product-compliance
Lightning Source LLC
Chambersburg PA
CBHW071435160426
43195CB00013B/1916